ECONOMIC CHANGES IN THE BAKING INDUSTRY

Supplement to BAKING IN AMERICA

Economic Changes in the Baking Industry

BY

CHARLES C. SLATER

Published as a supplement to *Baking in America,*
Northwestern University Press,
Evanston, Illinois, 1956

AMERICAN BAKERS ASSOCIATION

CHICAGO, ILLINOIS • 1958

Published as a Supplement to
BAKING IN AMERICA

NORTHWESTERN UNIVERSITY PRESS
EVANSTON, ILLINOIS, 1956

Library of Congress Catalog Card Number 58-14165

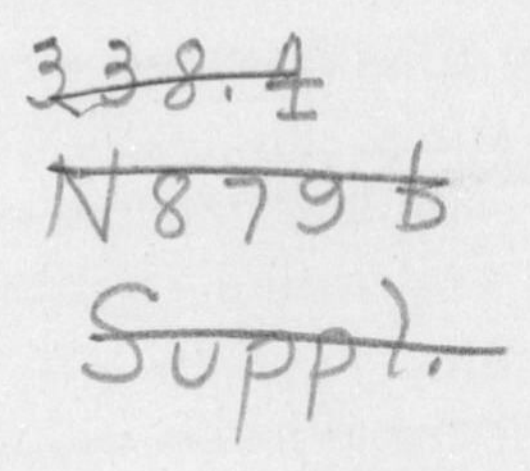

PRINTED IN THE UNITED STATES OF AMERICA
BY AMERICAN BOOK–STRATFORD PRESS, INC., NEW YORK

PREFACE

It was the wish of the American Bakers Association that the general economic study, *Baking in America,* developed at Northwestern University under a grant from the Association, be supplemented by further research as important new information came to light. The release of the *Census of Manufactures* of 1954 as well as other new fact-finding reports about the baking industry was such an occasion. This study was sponsored by the American Bakers Association to accomplish that purpose. For the author it was a challenging opportunity to reappraise findings and chart the changes in this dynamic industry since the publication of *Baking in America.*

It is the author's hope that the work will serve as a supplement to the earlier and larger work as well as provide the opportunity to check the direction and strength of trends revealed in the previous study. The work was undertaken with the same conditions of complete freedom of academic decision as the previous study. The author circulated the manuscript to the same panel of industry leaders who examined the early drafts of *Baking in America.* Thanks is due these industry executives, who all gave of their time to read the manuscript and give valuable critical advice. Among these readers Mr. Lloyd Wolfe was extremely helpful and untiring in his detailed and constructive criticism. The executives of the American Bakers Association contributed valuable assistance, among them Mr. Harold Fiedler and Mr. Donald Gerrish. The critical appraisal of the book has been extremely helpful, and the Association Committee asked that I make clear the fact that their review be in no way construed as a unanimous endorsement by the Association of all the statements contained in this book. This statement is important particularly in connection with new and unusual distribution systems described here. Since working at Northwestern University on *Baking In America,* the author was for over two years actively engaged in establishing some new bakery distribution programs while employed by Omar, Inc. This experience provided many insights into bakery operations and distribution problems, but I have endeavored here to remain as impartial as possible in discussing distribution practices. Many have helped the author but responsibility for form and content remain fully my own.

CHARLES C. SLATER
Glenview, Illinois

TABLE OF CONTENTS

LIST OF TABLES

LIST OF CHARTS

PART I

THE CHANGING ENVIRONMENT OF THE BAKING INDUSTRY

In the past few years, there has been definite evidence that the basic economic conditions facing the baking industry have been substantially modified. Changes in the organization of the industry will be examined, and an evaluation will be made of the industry responses to these external changes.

Demand Conditions

The trend of demand for bakery products over the past decade is an important determinant of the economic structure of the industry. Comparison of the actual pounds of bakery products shipped by industrial bakeries in 1947 and in 1954 gives us the most reliable measurement of the industry's actual performance in the period after World War II.

Chart I presents a comparison of the Census Reports for products shipped during these two bench mark years (1947 and 1954). The total of pounds shipped is up only 6 per cent over this period. Some important changes in the output of particular types of products are apparent. Variety breads are up 70 per cent in their production during this period; bread-type rolls are up 59 per cent; wheat breads are up 11 per cent. In contrast, rye and white breads are up only about 1 per cent.

This change does give the smaller baker in any given

market some increase in sales opportunity. Typically, the smaller plants tend to develop market niches in the production of specialty breads, relative to sale of the major loaf of white pan bread, the bulk of which is produced by the large bakery plants in any given market. The shift should not be overemphasized, however, for the relative importance of white bread is such as to dwarf the growth in sales of these variety breads. In fact, white pan bread dropped only from 74 per cent of all bread sales to about 70 per cent over this period of time.

Sweet goods are up only 1 per cent, while breads are up a full 7 per cent. There has been little change in the sale of sweet rolls, while pie and doughnut sales are up substantially and cookie and cake products sales are down. Pie and doughnut production has tended to become the province of the specialized bakery in many markets and of the newly emerged specialty *frozen* bakery product sellers. These shifts in preference should reveal their impact upon bakery producers, in the shifts in relative importance of various types of bakeries.

Another useful and interesting measure of output of the baking industry is the *Trend of Production of Bread and Other Yeast Raised Products.*[1] This report is published weekly by the American Bakers Association and summarized annually. It provides a trend series that is available continuously and supplements the more detailed information

---

[1] The weekly report is circulated to the firms participating in the task of providing weekly poundage sales information for the report each week and converted to an index of production for four regions of the country as well as a national average index of production. The Association reports that the data "are constructed from data submitted weekly by bakers producing over 80 million pounds of bread a week. The figures are tabulated as they are received to determine the per cent of increase or per cent of decrease in pounds produced from week to week.

It should be pointed out that the purpose of this material is to determine the trend of production over a given period of time. It is not designed to determine the total amount of bread produced in the nation. The poundage reported for this service each week by those who participated amounts to almost 25 per cent of all the bread produced for sale by all bakeries and chain stores each week. A sample as large as this, almost 25 per cent (with proper geographic distribution, which we have), is considered by statisticians to be more than adequate for trend determination purposes. Bakers that now participate use these figures to check their own bread production each week with the production of other companies."

CHART I

TOTAL POUNDS OF BAKERY PRODUCTS SHIPPED
1947 vs. 1954
(Comparison of Industry Totals)

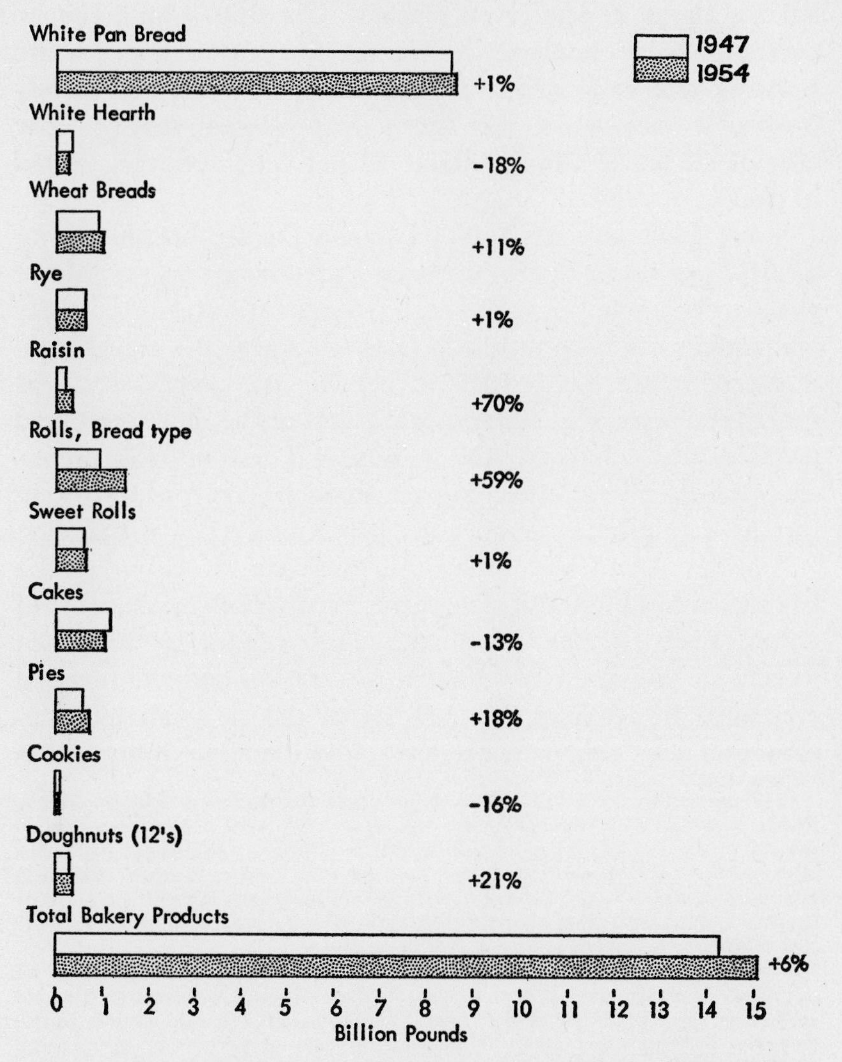

Source: *Census of Manufactures, 1954, Bakery Products,* Bulletin MC-20E, Table 6A (Washington, D. C.: Department of Commerce, Bureau of Census, 1956).

that is available every few years from the Census. The American Bakers Association trend data showed an increase in pounds produced of about 7½ per cent from 1947 to 1954. In contrast, the Census revealed a 6 per cent change over the same period. This very small difference certainly indicates that the American Bakers Association panel reports are a reliable indicator of the trend of output of the industry. The 1954 annual average index reported was 108.7 (with the 1947 index value equal to 100); the 1955 index was 109.7 and 1956 index was 111.9. There appears to be no substantial difference between the Census bench marks–showing a 6 per cent increase over the period–and the results from the American Bakers series. It would seem that the same trend of production is continuing since the Census of 1954.

An industry changes its output only in response to the aggregate demand for its products. But it is equally important to examine the per capita sale of the industry's product to determine more accurately the trend of the industry's development and its relative position with respect to other industries. Chart II presents the average per capita shipments of bakery products for the two Census years of 1947 and 1954. It can be seen that the per capita sales of industrial bakeries are down over five pounds during this seven year period. The per capita sale of white pan bread has dropped almost six pounds during this period, which explains most of the drop in per capita sales. Cakes, sweet rolls, rye bread, and cookie products have declined in per capita sale, too. The only significant sales increase on a per capita basis is in the product class of bread-type rolls, up over two and one-half pounds. Thus, it can be seen in Chart II that the total decline in per capita sales is about 6 per cent. Bread sales are down only 5 per cent while sweet product sales per person are down about 11 per cent.

Here are some factors behind this shift. It has been apparent for some years that the prepared cake mixes have cut

CHART II

ANNUAL PER CAPITA SALES OF BAKERY PRODUCTS OF VARIOUS TYPES

1947 vs. 1954

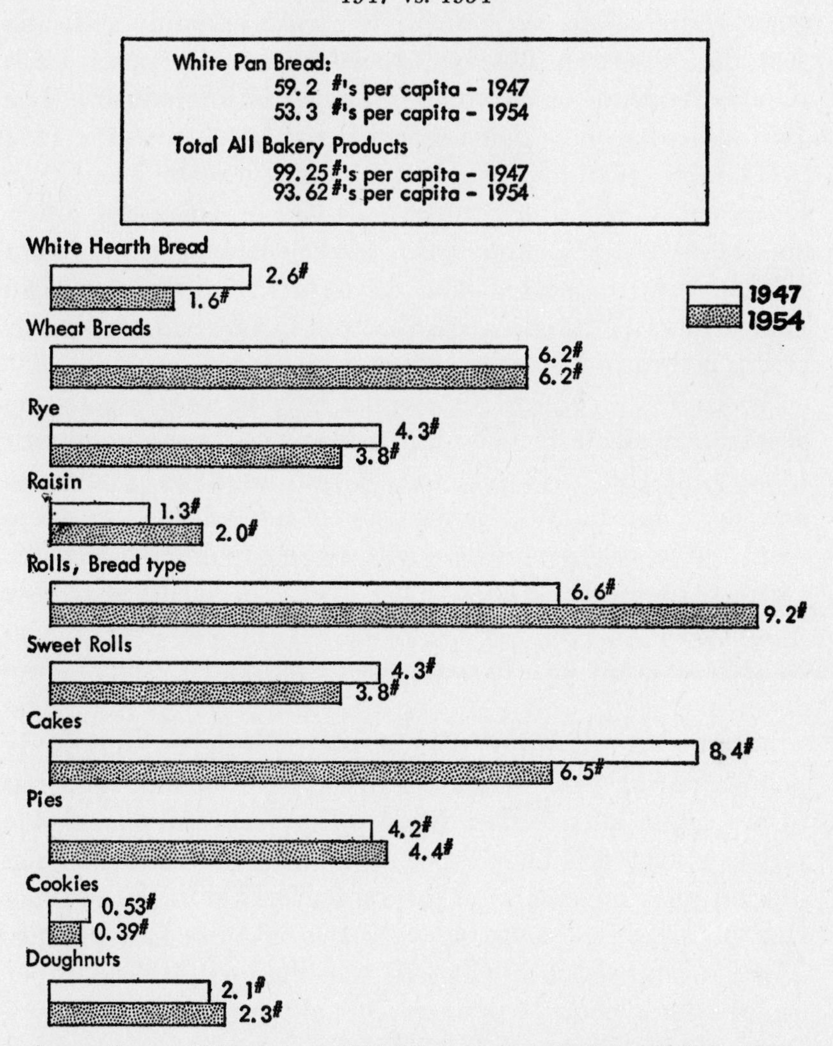

Source: *Census of Manufactures, 1954, Bakery Products,* Bulletin MC-20E, Table 6A (Washington, D. C.: Department of Commerce, Bureau of Census, 1956), pp. 13-14.

into cake sales.[2] Cake sales per capita have fallen, while another class of products that has been modified to make home preparation easier (frozen unbaked pies) has unquestionably produced an increase in *sales per person* during this same time period. Brown-N-Serve rolls and sandwich buns have been found to be an effective substitute for white breads. The growth in consumption of these products offsets nearly half the decline in sales of white bread.

On the basis of pounds of products shipped per person, all types of bakeries show some decline, except the chain store captive bakeries. On the basis of per capita shipments of product, the multi-outlet retail bakeries were the hardest hit, home service bakeries next and wholesale bakeries least of the three negatively affected bakery operations.

The analysis thus far gives us insights into what demand factors are working on the industry, but a direct examination of the comparative shares of pounds of products sold by the different distributive segments of the industry shows the impact of the changes on each type of operation.

Examination of Chart III shows that wholesale bakeries have gained about 1 per cent in their share of production, with a very slight shift in the ratio of bread products to other types of products. Home service bakeries have experienced some drop in market share. In 1954 home service bakeries dropped 1 to 1½ per cent in market share. Bread's share of home service products rose by almost 4 per cent. Meanwhile, chain store captive plants rose almost 3 per cent in their share of the total output, but experienced less than a 1 per cent decline in their share of the non-bread products sold. Comparisons for the multi-outlet retail bakeries are less meaningful than for other types of bakeries because of the changes in

---

[2] The shipment of all prepared flour mixes has risen from 8.85 pounds per capita in 1947 to 10.4 pounds per capita in 1954 (1,270,100,000 pounds to 1,676,200,000 pounds). The increase very nearly offsets the drop in bakery cake sales. See *1954 Census of Grain Mill Products,* Bulletin 20-D (Washington, D. C.: Bureau of the Census, Department of Commerce, 1956), p. 13.

CHART III

POUNDS OF BAKERY PRODUCT SHIPPED BY EACH MAJOR TYPE OF DISTRIBUTOR

1947 vs. 1954

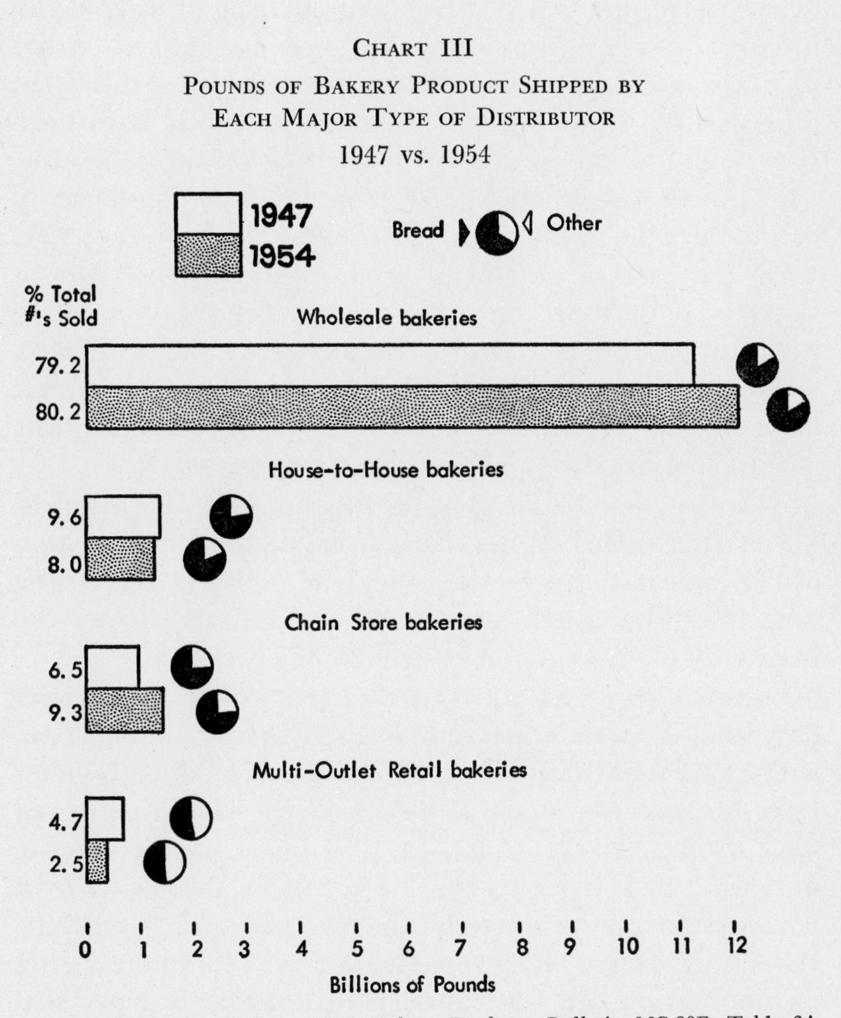

a. *Census of Manufactures, 1954, Bakery Products,* Bulletin MC-20E, Table 6A, *op. cit.*

b. Wholesale bakeries in 1947 classification included institutional bakeries as well.

c. Multi-outlet bakeries are not fully equivalent in the two censuses.

classification of the two Censuses.[3] In comparing only the shift in the types of products sold, bread sales are down for this group, in contrast to other types of bakeries.

Two other interesting items of evidence about the character of demand of bakery products have become available in the recent past: the Department of Agriculture's fine study, *Food Consumption of Households in the United States* and the two editions of the J. Walter Thompson Consumers Panel *Report on Baked Food Purchases,* March 1955, and March 1956.[4] Analysis of these studies helps us to understand the factors contributing to the changes in demand observed between the bench mark years of the *Census of Manufactures* and gives even more current data about the characteristic changes in the demand for baked goods.

Charts IV and V present some of the data contained in the U.S.D.A. study in a form that is comparable to the information presented in the 1948 study conducted by the U. S. Department of Agriculture.[5] The per family expenditures for bakery products are shown for three types of families, urban,

---

[3] Because of a change in definition in the Census of 1954, we should be cautious in drawing conclusions about the shifts in output and sales volume particularly in examining the retail multi-outlet bakeries. The Census of 1954 reports the following: "For 1954, all establishments producing bakery products primarily for direct sale to consumers on the premises were classified in retail trade, Industry 5462, and not in Industry 2051. The definition followed in the 1947 Census differs slightly in that an establishment producing for sale on the premises was included in Industry 2051 if it was part of a chain of such bakeries, but excluded if it was a single unit bakery. The 1947 statistics have not been revised to reflect this change in definition. Comparability between 1947 and 1954 is not significantly affected for Industry 2051, but the effect in statistics for the sub-industry, "retail multi-outlet bakeries," is greater. The apparent decreases in the sub-industry from 1947 to 1954 are believed to be due largely to this change in definition." U.S. Department of Commerce, Bureau of the Census, 1954 *Census of Manufactures, Bakery Products,* Bulletin MC-20E, Washington, D. C., 1956, p. 1.

[4] U.S. Department of Agriculture *Food Consumption of Households in the United States,* Household Food Consumption Survey, 1955, Report No. 1, Washington, D. C., and J. Walter Thompson Advertising Agency's Report entitled *Fleischmann Presents a Consumer Panel Report on Baked Food Purchases* March 1956, Second Annual Edition. Circulated privately by the Standard Brands Company of New York.

[5] See page 59, Volume II, *Baking in America,* and for original source U. S. Department of Agriculture, *Food Consumption of Urban Families with Children and Families with no Children, United States, Spring 1948.* Preliminary Report No. 14 (Washington: U. S. Department of Agriculture, January 1950), p. 5.

CHART IV

DOLLAR VALUE OF BAKERY PRODUCT PURCHASES (One Week, April-June, 1955) URBAN, RURAL NON-FARM AND FARM FAMILIES OF 2 OR MORE PERSONS

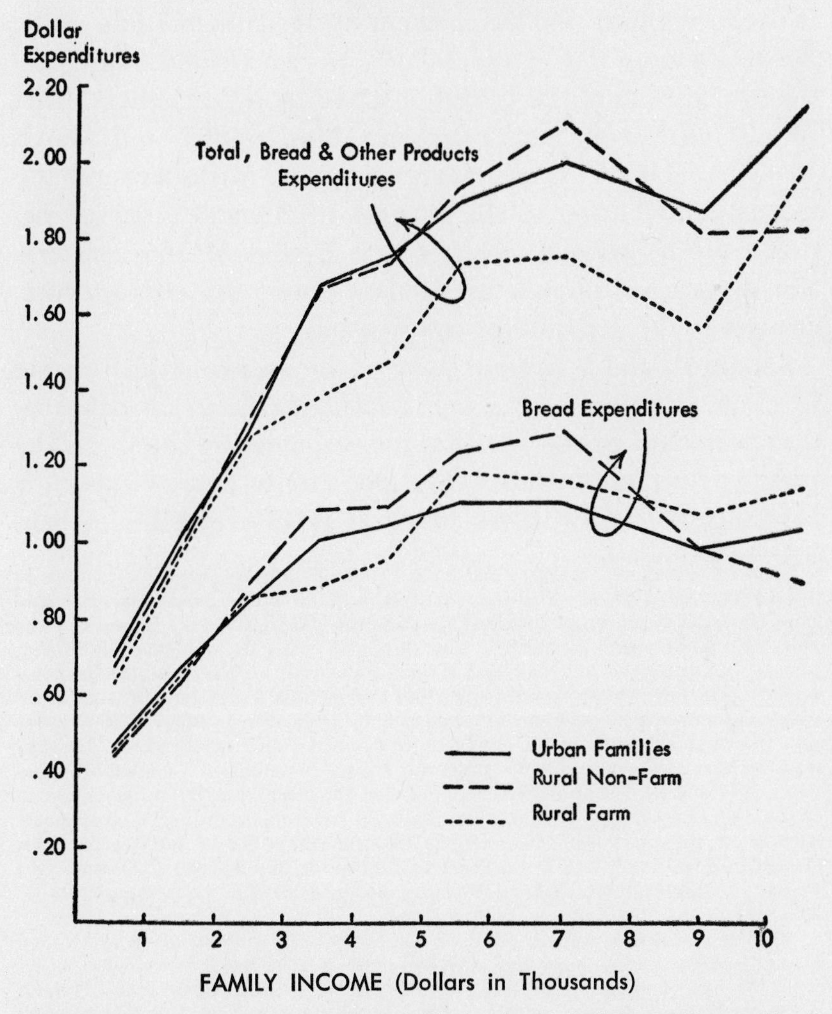

Source: *Food Consumption of Households in the United States.* Report No. 1 (Washington, D. C.: Department of Agriculture, 1956), p. 62 and following.

CHART V

POUNDS OF BAKERY PRODUCTS CONSUMED BY HOUSEHOLDS OF VARIOUS INCOME LEVELS

(During one week period, April-June, 1955)

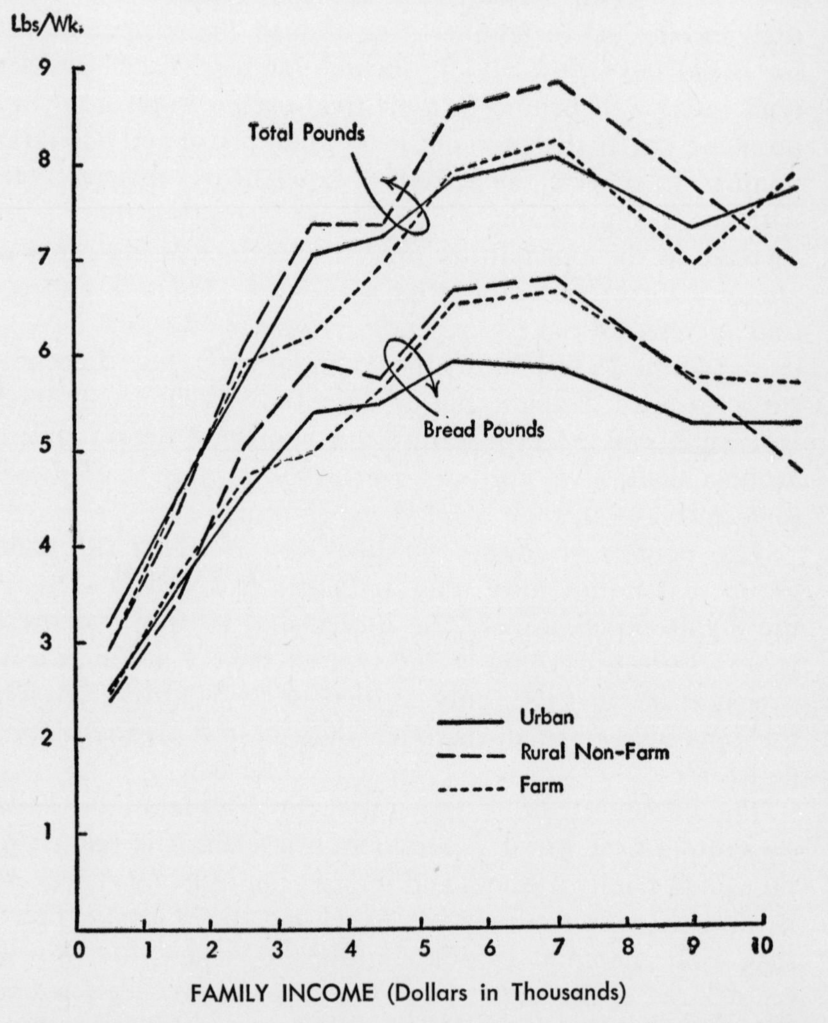

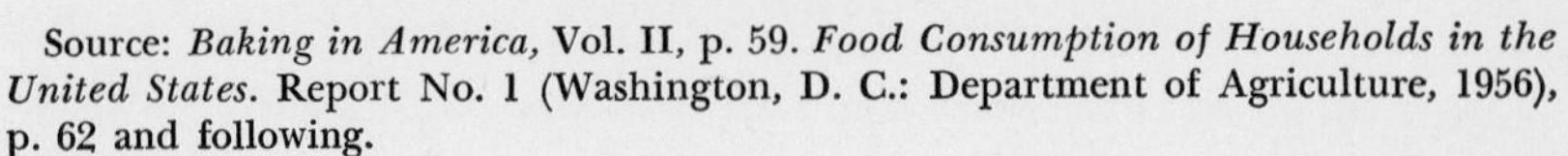

Source: *Baking in America,* Vol. II, p. 59. *Food Consumption of Households in the United States.* Report No. 1 (Washington, D. C.: Department of Agriculture, 1956), p. 62 and following.

rural non-farm and farm, and these three types of families are subdivided into the various income levels reported. The variations in their expenditures show some interesting contrasts with the information presented about families in the 1948 study. Top spenders for all bakery products are the high income urban families even though their expenditures for bread fall below middle income families. Farm families tend to lag well behind in their total expenditures, but they do spend nearly the same on bread as do urban and non-farm families. In general, the pattern of expenditures changes more with the income among the non-bread items, but there is an increase in the expenditure for bread as income rises that is almost a direct and proportional increase. There is a three-fold increase in bakery expenditures for a four-fold income rise until the $5,000 family income level is reached. Expenditures for bread begin to fall off after the $7,000 income level is reached, and the expenditures for non-bread items stabilize at this income level until the over $10,000 group again shows some increases in their level of expenditure.

The pounds of bakery products consumed by the same group of families show only a slightly flattened level from the dollar expenditures. The implication is clear that there is very little upgrading of the type of bakery products consumed as incomes rise, only an increase in quantity of nearly the same types of products rather than more expensive bakery delicacies.

The inference can be drawn that the decline in per capita consumption of bread reported by the Census is related to the rise in family incomes and the fact that the higher income families actually consume less bread and spend less for bread than more moderate income families. A further inference to be deduced is that bakery producers may have neglected to upgrade products to capture the appetites of higher income families, as indicated by the fact that the high income families buy products that cost only slightly more per pound than do the lower income families.

Somewhat more detailed information about consumer expenditures is contained in the Fleischmann Report. Chart VI shows the expenditures for all bakery products, per month, for families of different size.[6] As might be expected, families with children are the largest bakery product purchasers, and the more children, the more bakery goods bought. The larger families do not maintain as high a per capita expenditure as do the smaller families with a higher proportion of adults in the family group. This study confirms a number of things about consumption patterns that are almost common knowledge. The evidence of consumption increases as family increases is in substantial agreement with the Department of Agriculture study. There is a difference in the per family expenditure for bakery products reported by these two independently conducted studies of food expenditures. The difference is not easily reconciled, since the techniques of sampling and reporting of both groups are statistically well regarded. The expenditures reported by the Department of Agriculture studies are about 20 per cent higher than those reported by the Fleischmann studies. This disparity in aggregate expenditures reported assumes less importance when the reports are used for comparisons within each report, such as variations in expenditure among income classes, family size groups or geographical areas.

Regional variations in consumption are in agreement with the data presented in the Census Reports. The most interesting phases of the Report provide a picture of the patterns of shopping habits for bakery products. The study reveals that about 46 per cent of all bakery products are actually purchased on Fridays and Saturdays. Slightly less bread is bought (proportionately) than rolls, sweet goods, cake and pie products.

Conclusions to be drawn from consumption data are that the total output of the industry has risen slightly, but the

---

[6] *Fleischmann Presents a Consumer Panel Report on Baked Foods Purchases,* Standard Brands, Inc. (New York, 1956), p. 3.

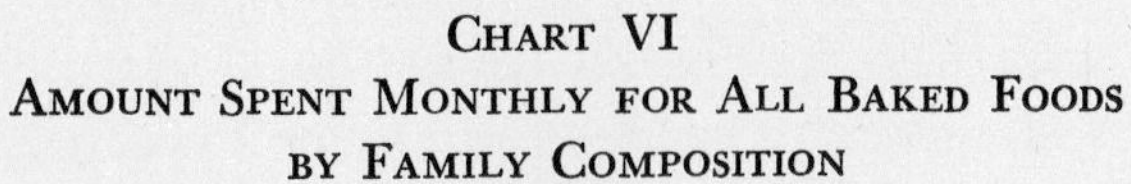

CHART VI
AMOUNT SPENT MONTHLY FOR ALL BAKED FOODS
BY FAMILY COMPOSITION

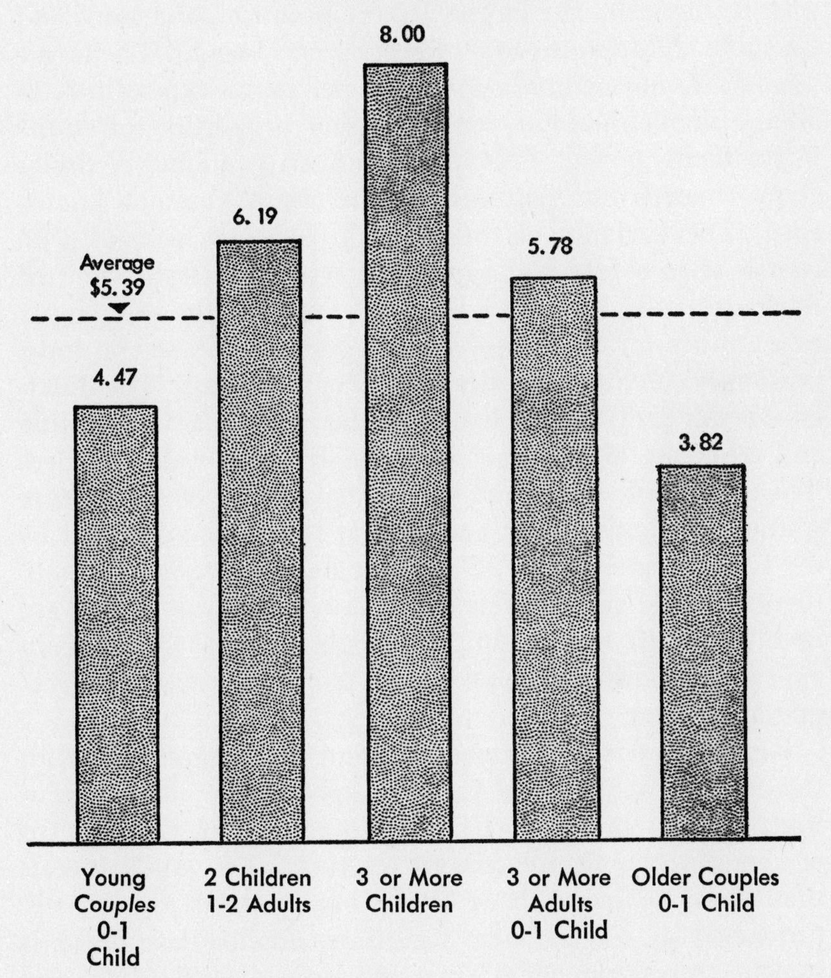

Source: *Fleischmann Presents a Consumer Panel Report on Baked Foods Purchases* (New York: Standard Brands, Inc., 1956).

per capita sale of bakery products has, in fact, declined at a rate of 1 per cent per year! The sharp differences in the rate of consumption of families of different income levels help explain the decline. The higher income families actually consume fewer pounds of bakery products, particularly breads, than do the middle income families. The rise in real incomes during the past few years has put a larger per cent of the families in this country into this high income group, which for bakery products means a lower level of consumption. A comparison of Charts IV and V shows a slight difference in unit cost of products among the lower income families than the higher income families. This then reveals that the industry may not have provided sufficient attractive products of higher cost that tempt the high income families to purchase bakery products rather than other types of non-bakery foods.

Changing Shopping Habits Have Impact on Bakery Operation

Because bakery product sales constitute less than 5 per cent of the total retail sales in most food stores, it is almost axiomatic that the changes in shopping habits affecting food stores will have a direct effect on wholesale and chain store captive plant bakeries, and indirectly an effect upon other distributive channels for bakery products.[7] Food distribution has changed in the past few years due to horizontal and vertical concentration in food distribution.

Fewer larger stores now serve consumers who are willing to travel farther to reach these larger outlets—in effect, a horizontal concentration of food sales outlets. The trend toward supermarket distribution has, of course, gone on for some time.

Supermarkets increased in number from 16,540 in 1952 to 27,000 in 1956. In these four years their share of total

---

[7] *This Week Magazine 6th Biennial Grocery Study* (prepared for limited circulation by *This Week Magazine,* 1955, United Newspaper Corp.) reports that bakery sales constitute 2.67% of food store sales in supermarkets studied.

grocery store sales has jumped from 43.8 per cent to 62 per cent.[8] This has had a marked effect on the baking business. Fewer larger stores are not served as well by traditional wholesale distribution of bakeries as were the many small food stores in the past.

The distributive system for wholesale bakeries is designed to serve stores of homogeneous size. The growing disparity in size of food stores, of course, reflects the demands of homemakers to shop the more economical, wider assortment offered by the supermarket. The 27,000 supermarkets in 1956 amounted to only 8.7 per cent of all grocery and combination meat and grocery stores; yet as was just pointed out, they accounted for 62 per cent of the forty-two and one-half billion dollars in food store sales.

Of probably even greater significance to the baking industry is the pattern of change that has occurred in the vertical concentration of food distribution. The chain food organization is centered on the coordinated buying and marketing activity at the warehouse level. When unable to buy on favorable terms, chain organizations have often resorted to having their own label produced by outside manufacturers and to going into the manufacturing business on their own; baking is an excellent example of this vertical concentration activity.

Table 1 sets out some facts of real interest on this point. Chains of eleven or more stores account for only 5.8 per cent of all grocery stores, yet they do over 36 per cent of all food store sales. Earlier it was shown that their captive baking plants had gained 2.8 per cent of the market in pounds produced from the years of 1947 through 1954, although the share of the total food sales done by chain food organizations has remained remarkably stable over the last decade.

Among independent food stores, over 32 per cent of all outlets are now members of voluntary buying groups or cooperatives. These affiliated stores do 44 per cent of all volume

---

[8] 1957 Edition, 24th Annual Survey, *Facts in Grocery Distribution* (New York: *Progressive Grocer,* 1957), p. 3.

TABLE 1

STRUCTURE OF FOOD RETAILING

Number of Outlets and Sales Volume of Various Classifications[a]

	Sales			Number of Outlets		
	$'s in 1956 (in millions)	*% of Total*		*Number*	*% of Total*	
Types of Outlets		*Groc. & Comb. Only*	*Total*		*Groc. & Comb. Only*	*Total*
Grocery & Comb. Stores						
Chains (11 or more)	$15,500	36.4%	32.7%	18,000	5.8%	4.5%
Independent						
Affiliated Stores[b]	18,925	44.6	40.0	90,000	29.0	22.5
Unaffiliated Stores	8,075	19.0	17.0	202,000	65.2	50.3
Total Grocery & Comb. Stores	$42,500	100.%	...	310,000	100.%	...
Specialty Stores (Chain and Independent)	4,900		10.3	91,000		22.7
	$47,400		100.0%	401,000		100.0%

[a] Source: 1957 Edition, 24th Annual Survey, *Facts on Grocery Distribution* (New York: *Progressive Grocer,* 1957), p. 1.

[b] Includes buying co-operative members and stores supplied by so-called cost-plus warehouses.

done by independent food stores. This leaves only 19 per cent of the grocery store sales volume that is done by stores that are independent of both chain or voluntary and co-operative alliance, yet these small independent food stores still constitute roughly two-thirds of all grocery stores. Thus, the "mom 'n pop" stores have not disappeared as yet, although their importance in food distribution is fading rapidly. The significance of this information to the baking industry lies in the fact that wholesale bakeries are serving food stores of such difference in size and of such great variation in their vertical relationship with their primary warehouse supplier and with a single method of bakery distribution—the commission paid driver who picks up surplus and places merchandise on display, collecting for it each day. It is a system designed for the smaller stores (which still constitute the majority of all outlets but do not account for the majority of food store sales or bakery product sales).

The impact of the growing importance of the affiliations of independent food stores to the merchandising and warehousing centers that serve them should not be underestimated. The warehouse, to justify existence and to present countervailing power to meet the impact of low priced chain brands, must offer member stores products that the chain offers at comparable cost. The greater the volume of products that flow through the central billing service of the warehouse, the lower the unit cost of landing groceries at the retail level.

Thus, it is not just the independent food stores that demand bakery products, indeed all products, at costs comparable to chain costs—but the large and efficient warehousing-merchandising center that supplies millions of dollars worth of food stuffs to hundreds of stores in any given area. Often these independent warehousing operations have average operating costs that are not in excess of those incurred by chain operators in the same markets. The independent food warehouse (voluntary or co-operative) is a financially powerful and competent champion of the independent stores' demands on manufacturers. In many lines, the affiliated groups have proven as competent as their chain counterparts in extracting favorable terms from manufacturers. Indeed, the very large chains cannot risk the sharp competitive practices common to many smaller organizations both chain or independent, for fear of public or government disapproval.

Some interesting and pertinent data on this is contained in Professor Paul D. Converse's "Twenty-five Years of Wholesaling: A Revolution in Food Wholesaling," in the July 1, 1957, issue of *Journal of Marketing*. Converse explains the changes in thinking that have affected independent food stores and wholesale houses:

> There has been a revolution in the distribution of food since 1920. In 1920, a grocery product costing the wholesaler $1.00 would usually cost the retailer $1.13 and the consumer $1.40. Today this item will reach the consumer at about $1.20 if purchased in a modern supermarket. . . .
>
> If they were going to survive, they had to find out what the chains did and do it equally well or better. If the retailers went out of business, so would the wholesalers. To stay in business, the wholesalers had to save the retailers. To save the retailers, two things were necessary: the retailers must be able to buy their goods at lower prices and the retailers had to operate better stores. . . .
>
> A recent count showed 456 voluntary wholesalers with 89,000 affiliated retailers. They are called "voluntaries" because the retailers voluntarily affiliate with them. The basic idea of the voluntary wholesaler is that he secures a group of retailers who buy all or most of their goods from him, and, in return, he furnishes them with merchandising assistance in operating their stores and gives them a franchise to use the sponsor's name on their stores. This may be a nationally controlled name like IGA, Red and White, or Clover Farm or a name the wholesaler controls as Super Valu, Royal Blue, Jack Spratt, or Cardinal.

Of prime significance to the baking industry is the fact that the wider the line offered by the wholesaler, the lower the overall cost is likely to be. All perishables are falling into this new distributive channel. Food chains led the way and have long since been a poor market for bakery manufacturers, but as independent stores fall into this pattern, distributive changes for bakery products loom in importance.

Converse presents the operating details of one major cost-plus house, Super Valu Stores, Inc.

> The operations of a voluntary grocery wholesaler may be illustrated with the business of Super Valu Stores, Inc., of

> Hopkins, Minnesota, and other towns in Iowa and North and South Dakota. . . . It operated for years in a multistory warehouse in the orthodox way as a service wholesaler. It sent salesmen to the retailers to solicit business and sold them on credit. . . . Chain-store competition became keen in this area in the 1920's, and in 1932 Winston & Newell secured a group of independent retailers to affiliate with them and organized a voluntary chain. . . . In 1932 the company had 5,400 customers and sales of $4,500,000. Today the company sells approximately $100,000,000 to 570 affiliated retail stores. . . .

The story of Super Valu is repeated across the country by both voluntary, cost-plus houses and co-ops. It is a case of vertical integration to meet the food chains that have integrated vertically—after achieving control of retail outlets by horizontal integration of many retail food stores. The manufacturer of branded food items has found it increasingly difficult to provide products to the 65 per cent of all food stores that account for a shrinking segment (still 19 per cent of sales) and yet to deal effectively with chains and affiliated stores that account for 81 per cent of food store sales with only 35 per cent of the outlets.

The crux of the matter is in the marketing policy of branded manufacturers who try to prevent distributive groups from dominating their price and display policies by selling on equal terms to large and small buyer alike. Chain and affiliated store groups neither need nor want the marketing service of the branded seller, but they want the saving passed on that elimination of sales staff and promotion would mean.

Another interesting point of comparision of more direct relationship to the baking industry revolves around the share of bakery sales done by chains in specific markets. Two items of information are relevant: first, the data on consumer buying habits for the city of Chicago, and second, projection data on private or controlled label bread sales. These data illustrate the market share enjoyed by the store-controlled brands of white bread.[9]

The Chicago city data are provided by the excellent consumer panel diary sponsored by the Family Service Bureau of the *Chicago Tribune*.[10] The two sets of data are presented in conjunction here. Chart VII shows the continuous areas of the earlier as well as of the later data. The data are simplified here to present three broad categories, major wholesale brands, small wholesale and retail bakery brands, and chain controlled brands. Inspection reveals that major wholesaler brands held their aggregate share of the market until the beginning of 1956, even though chain controlled brands had gained in share of the white bread market at the expense of smaller wholesale companies and retail bake shops. In 1956, however, the chains continued their gain, but in this last year their gains have been at the expense of the major brands of bread. Thus, while Census information of 1954 shows that captive plant production of bakery products amounted to only 9 per cent of bread sales, the Chicago market reveals that it was closer to 25 per cent in 1954—and, in 1956, close to one-third of all white bread sold in the metropolitan area of Chicago. The discrepancy between Census figures and the *Chicago Tribune* data are explainable by two facts: 1.) Chain plants in Chicago have a higher, and growing, percentage of captive plant output than is true nationwide, and 2.) Some store groups are supplied by bakeries not primarily in the chain store bread business. This latter category seems to be of growing significance in many markets. A further interesting fact is the relative proportion of their own brand of bread sold in chain stores as opposed to wholesaler brands of bread.

---

[9] The term *private label* is used here to refer to products sold under the stores' own label. *Controlled label* may be supplied to the store without its ownership of the brand.

[10] E. J. Luby of the *Chicago Tribune* prepared market share brand constancy data for the author's earlier work. See pp. 89-96, *Baking in America,* Volume II. Similar data have been gathered for a later period through June 1956.

CHART VII

MARKET SHARE OF WHITE BREAD SALES IN METROPOLITAN CHICAGO

(November 1950 through June 1956)

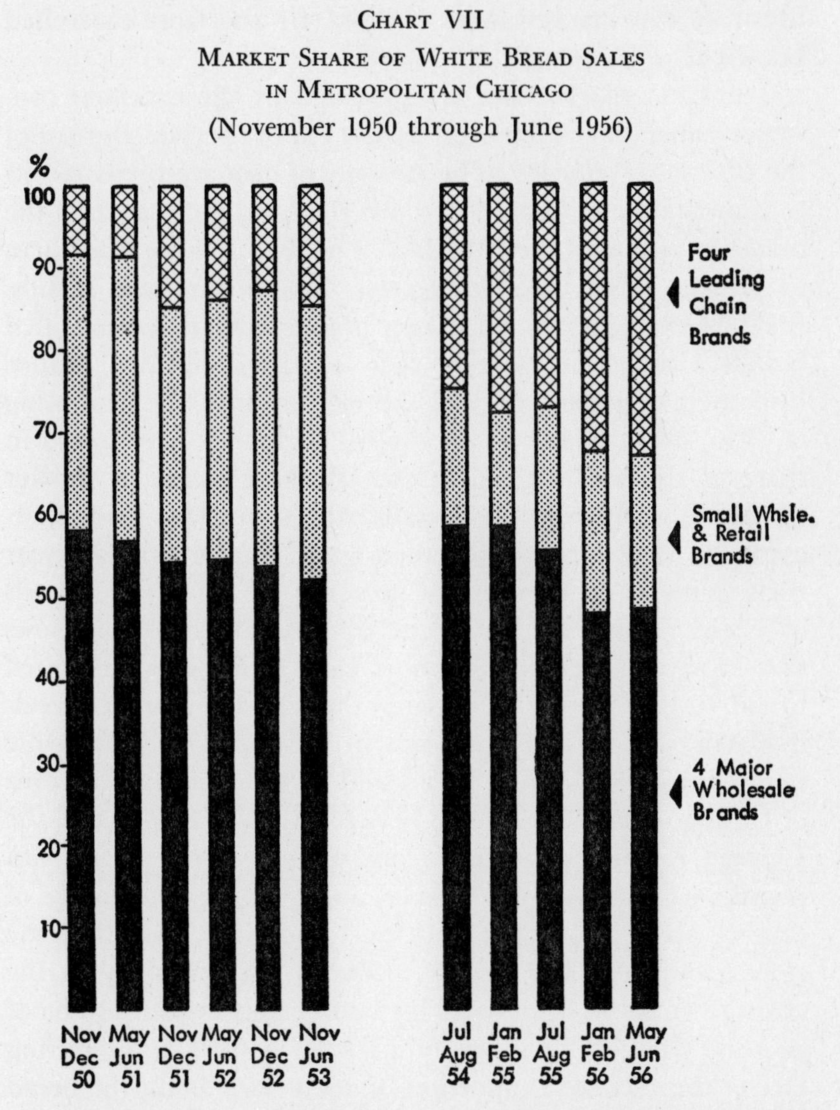

Source: *Chicago Tribune* Family Service Bureau, Chicago, Ill. Chains are A & P's Jane Parker, National's Top Taste, and after July 1954 includes Jewel Tea and Kroger. Wholesalers are Continental, Interstate, Ward and Gordon.

Table 2 shows that this share ranges from 52 per cent up to 91 per cent.

TABLE 2

RELATIVE SHARE OF OWN BRAND OF PRE-WRAPPED WHITE BREAD SOLD IN LEADING CHAIN STORES IN CHICAGO *

May–June 1956

Chain Store	*Share of Own Brand Sold*
A & P	91.7%
National Tea	72.4%
Kroger	70.6%
Jewel Tea	52.8%

* Source: *Chicago Tribune* Family Service Bureau, Chicago, Illinois.

This information can be related to some other interesting evidence on the current importance of captive plant and private label bread sales through food stores and the probable trends of this method of selling.

First, Standard Brands released a report of the purchasing habits of over 6,000 families in the J. Walter Thompson Consumer Panel titled *Fleischmann Presents a Consumer Panel Report on Baked Foods Purchases for March 1955.* This report was referred to earlier. In that report an analysis was made of where bread was purchased. It was reported that for a one month period Panel families spent 81¢ on bread in chain stores and $1.23 on bread in all other food stores. This means that chain stores are selling almost 40 per cent of the bread bought in food stores. Of course, not all of this bread is their own label, but evidence from the *Chicago Tribune* Consumer Panel indicates that this share would range between 50 per cent and 90 per cent, cited just above. Thus, this estimate of private label would be between 20 per cent and 36 per cent of all white bread if all chains had their own private label. We can examine other public information which will lead us to form other estimates of the importance of private label.

The *National Bread Price Survey* of May 1, 1956, compiled by the Anheuser-Busch Company of St. Louis gives an estimate of the number of chain organizations that sell bread at a price lower than the price prevailing on the market among bakery organizations supplying the grocery trade. There were, in that issue of the Survey, 58 chain food organizations offering price bread. They account for 13,528 food stores.[11] This is more than 65 per cent of all chain food store outlets. There is every reason to believe that these chain stores do a disproportionately large share of the total of all chain store business. Generally, it is the larger chain store organizations that have their own bread plants or acquire private label merchandise for their store outlets.

Progressive Grocer's 1956 Report, *Facts on Grocery Distribution*, declares that there were 18,800 food stores in chain store organizations of eleven or more stores during that year, and that they did about 36 per cent of all food store sales.[12]

Relating these three items of evidence cited, we might assume that 65 per cent of the chain stores featuring low price bread do approximately three-fourths of all the chain store sales. From this we can estimate the volume of private label bread sales. This means that the chain food stores offering their own private label bakery products account for no less than 25 per cent (i.e., 75 per cent of 36 per cent of all food store sales). This more round-about approach yields a figure that is 13 per cent less than the highest figures of the Fleischmann Report, and there are several reasons to believe that this total might be conservative. Failure to be reported either in the Anheuser-Busch Bread Price Survey or in the

---

[11] Based on the tabulation of the number of stores operated by each store organization reported in the Survey according to the 1956 "Directory of Super Markets and Grocery Chains" published by Business Guides, Incorporated, a *Chain Store Age* affiliate, New York, New York.

[12] 1956 Edition, 23rd Annual Survey, *Facts on Grocery Distribution* (New York: *Progressive Grocer*, 1956).

Chain Store Age Directory would mean being overlooked in this estimate of the total, but there is less likelihood of error in the other direction. Moreover, independent food stores, such as members of voluntary chains or cooperatives, are not counted in this total of stores selling private label or price bread.

Thus, there is substantial evidence which indicates that at least one-third of all bread sold in food stores is sold under the private label of chain food stores or voluntary chains or co-op members. In contrast to this situation, the *Census of Manufactures* of 1947 showed that only 90 chain store bakery plants were in operation, and that they produced an estimated total of only 6½ per cent of all bread sold through food stores. By 1954 the *Census of Manufactures* reported that the share of captive plant bread production was 9.3 per cent of the pounds of all bread sold. Thus, even a sharp acceleration in the development of privately controlled plants would not account for the substantial difference or spread between the chain store-owned plants sales of 1954 and the total of price bread or private or controlled label bread sold in 1956. We must conclude that a substantial share of the bakery products sold under private label by chains is purchased from bakery plants not owned by the chain.

From the evidence cited here, we can conclude that the last few years have seen a substantial increase in the pressures toward horizontal integration of food retailing outlets. This has increased the relative efficiency of captive plant bakery operations of food organizations or their private label distribution, as opposed to the efficiency of the traditional wholesaling methods of bakeries serving individual food stores with commission-paid drivers and pick-up of surplus merchandise. Of equal or perhaps even greater importance is the increasing importance of captive plant operations and the private label bakery products turned out for chains, voluntary chains and cooperatives. This backward vertical integration of food distributing organizations into acquiring control of manufacturing facilities in the bakery field has its parallel in other perishable product fields, but it has had an important impact on the competitive practices and distributive systems of the perishable bakery products industry.

Technological Factors Inducing Changes in the Economics of the Baking Industry

Up to this point the report has concentrated upon the *demand* forces that have worked to modify the organization and operation of the baking industry in the recent past; of equal economic significance are the forces affecting *supply*. Two factors are important here, the advent of new techniques and the changes in the relative cost of input factors such as raw materials, supplies and labor. Let's review each of these elements in the supply side of the baking industry in turn.

The techniques of bakery production have changed recently. The most notable advance has been in improvement in storage abilities. Of particular significance is the freezing of bakery products. At the time of the author's earlier writing the application of freezing was limited, but widespread experimentation was under way. Today many plants freeze finished bakery products.[13] The primary advantage of freezing has been to equalize work loads by producing to inventory rather than to the sharply fluctating demands experienced day by day in the industry.

In brief, here is a typical application for industrial freezers in baking of non-bread items. Weekly anticipated orders for varieties of cakes, dark breads and pastry items are assembled. Those items which can be successfully frozen are selected for runs for the whole week rather than for daily use. The merchandise is produced for freezer inventory. Two immediate

---

[13] For some detailed information on this development see *Baking Industry* Magazine, Clissold Publishing Company, Chicago, particularly: Derby, Thomas H., "What's Ahead for Frozen Bakery Foods," Jan. 29, 1955, p. 33; Hatherly, Chas. D., "Freezing Bakery Products is Paying Us Big Dividends," April 23, 1955, p. 42; "Arnold's Bakers, Inc., Port Chester, N. Y., New Bread Freezing Plant in Operation," Aug. 28, 1954, p. 69; A. Robinson, "Quick Freezing of Bakery Products," Dec. 15, 1956, p. 42.

advantages are felt: first, the longer runs of these items cut the unit cost involved in set-up and clean-up after each item is produced; second, the work schedule simplification cuts costs of overtime and permits better labor utilization.

The freezer inventory of prepackaged products can be held for several days or even weeks without sharp declines in quality. The daily requirements are brought from freezers directly to defrost chambers. The defrost chamber used in many plants is of a type that maintains low humidity and high temperature, so that the frozen products accumulate very little precipitated moisture during the short time required to raise the temperature from about –10 degrees Fahrenheit up to room temperature of 60 degrees to 80 degrees Fahrenheit. The defrost chamber is a special requirement of large quantity defrost problems; small quantites of frozen bakery products can be defrosted in well ventilated rooms, of course, but large quantities require the conditioned air of defrost chambers. Although bakery technologists with whom the author has discussed the subject do not agree precisely on the shelf-life reduction incurred through freezing, the stopping of the clock for these perishable products compensates for the slight reduction in shelf life experienced. Freezing provides further advantages to large plants, even permitting the shipment of frozen products to distant depots for defrost and sale at the distant market. The feasible radius of service for plants large enough to employ freezers has been expanded greatly by this technological innovation.

Many related inventions have been a necessary part of the modern technique of freezing of certain bakery products. Special freezer types of cellophane have come out; research in cereal chemistry in the use of bakery ingredients other than flour under these novel conditions is being explored. The bakery allied trades have been much more active in the development of products and supplies useful in freezing than have operating bakeries for the most part. In some cases, which will be cited later in discussions of the competitive patterns emerging, supplying allied trades have in fact emerged as distributors of frozen bakery products.

The application of temperature controlled bakery products which are sold in a frozen state or a refrigerated condition has grown in importance recently. Census figures reveal that manufacturers other than bakeries have grown in importance in the production of rolls, sweet yeast goods and pies from the period of 1947 to 1954. Table 3 shows the growth of output

TABLE 3

GROWTH OF NON-BAKING INDUSTRY OUTPUT OF SELECTED BAKERY PRODUCTS *

	Dollar Value of Shipments		*Pounds Shipped*	
	1947	*1954*	*1947*	*1954*
Bread Type Rolls	$ 437,000	$ 1,589,000	2,434,000	7,422,000
Sweet Yeast Goods	659,000	5,616,000	2,410,000	16,000,000
Pies	284,000	3,086,000	552,000	12,607,000
Total All Bread and Related Products	$10,170,000	$17,451,000	....	....

* Source: *Census of Manufactures, 1954, Bakery Products,* Table 6A, Bulletin MC-20E (Washington, D. C.: Department of Commerce, Bureau of Census, 1956), p. 15.

of selected bakery products by firms not primarily engaged in baking. When this rather sharp growth of non-baking industry entry into fields hitherto restricted to the baking industry is contrasted with the experience of bread and related products industries (defined as Industry 2051 by the Bureau of the Census), the changes are striking. The baking industry experienced roughly a one-sixth increase in the total output of pies during the period from 1947 to 1954, while the non-baking industry output of pie products was a twenty-four fold increase! [14]

Measured in pounds produced, there was slightly over a

[14] Major entrants in this field include soup manufacturers (Campbell Soup's Swanson Division), canned milk producers (Carnation and Pet Milk Co.'s), poultry processors (Blue Star Foods), and canners (such as Stokely, Van Camp), as well as one major bakery firm (Continental Baking Co., purchaser of Morton Packing Co.).

2 per cent increase in the production of sweet yeast goods for the baking industry from the period of 1947 to 1954, while the non-baking industry had an 800 per cent increase in the output of sweet yeast goods during the same period. Bread type rolls grew in importance in the baking industry measured in pounds by roughly 50 per cent, while non-baking industry output of equivalent types of products was close to 250 per cent. To a considerable extent the growth of the non-baking industry output of bakery products is in the field of frozen bakery goods. There is every reason to expect that the growth rate shown in the period from 1947 to 1954 has gone on at an even more rapid pace among non-baking industry firms during the three years that have elapsed since the census was taken.

Another change of primary importance in the techniques employed by the baking industry is the increased use of transport trailers. While transport trucks represent no major technological change in the methods of operation available to the baking industry, their extension in use relates to other technological distributive factors which make this increase in use of transport trucks of major significance in the technological changes of the industry. The number and distance from plant of depots for distribution have increased sharply since 1947. While general statistics are not available, individual items in evidence available to the author indicate that this technique of extending the distributive radius of plants has taken on much more widespread importance in the recent past.

The extensive use of bulk handling techniques for the delivery of raw ingredients to the mixing points in plants has risen in importance in the recent past. Again, no general statistics are available for the industry as a whole, but information indicates that this has become of much more widespread significance in the industry.[15]

---

[15] For further information see *Baking Industry* Magazine, *op. cit.*; Drever, Bruce J., June 5, 1954; June 19, 1954, p. 45. Also, August 11, 1956, issue for special report on "Bulk Handling."

The availability of freezing permits large plants to gain efficiencies in a wider line of product. Larger plants are more able to quickly utilize the increase in capitalization (to gain longer runs on high speed equipment) than are small plants that utilize extensive hand shop techniques. Similarly, the use of bulk handling techniques for ingredients and supplies has favored the larger plant where the capital investment is more fully warranted than in the smaller operation. The availability of truck transport and the reduced cost of operating transports over great distances have favored large plants that enjoy lower costs and are thus able to extend their market area rather than fight more intensively to gain market share in their home market.

These important technological changes seem to favor large plants and encourage concentration into the hands of fewer, larger plants with lower overall costs. These changes have also encouraged entry into the baking industry by primary material suppliers and others in related food processing industries that are able to capitalize on the growing market for frozen bakery products.

Changes in the Relative Importance of Factors of Cost to the Baking Industry

In addition to broad shifts in outlets and final buyer demand for bakery products, there are recent changes in cost experience.

Changes in the relative importance of specific factor costs can have a sharp impact on the relative prices necessary to cover production costs of specific items. Changes in factor costs bear a direct relationship to the price which must be charged for various types of products. This has an effect on the relative output of the different types of bakery producers.

Chart VIII, showing the trend of cost and profits for all industrial bakeries through the years 1947 to 1954, reveals that material costs have dropped from slightly over 54 per cent to slightly more than 49 per cent. Wage costs have been the primary factor which has risen relative to total bakery revenue over this period of time. The sharpest increase was during the period from 1949 to 1950, reflecting the increase in wage costs during the Korean War. The total wage bill of the baking industry has risen from 27¢ out of every dollar of revenue in 1947 to 32¢ in 1954. With the substitution of higher wages for falling material costs, other costs and profits have held about the same share of revenue, rising barely 1 per cent during the entire period.

Production wage costs have been more erratic in their changes over time as a percentage of all costs and profits, but the trend of change appears to match closely that of the balance of other wage costs, including distribution labor. The relative number of workers engaged in production tasks has fallen during the same period that is covered here, 1947 to 1954. An analysis based on the same data reveals that the percentage of production workers out of the total work force in the baking industry has shrunk from 64.2 per cent in 1947 to 58 per cent in 1954. The slight shift in total output of the industry was positive. Fewer production workers turn out more product today, and they receive a larger share per person of the total wage bill.

Improved plant equipment, particularly installation of freezers and better handling equipment, accounts for part of the drop in labor force. In addition, the shift of volume to large bakery plants that enjoy higher per man-hour output has explained part of the change. This cost shifting trend has played a role in modifying the structure of the industry.

Pertinent to this discussion of cost trends are the reports of both 18 multi-plant companies (covering between 397 and 417 plants for the different years) and the reports of 18 single plant companies (covering, of course, only 18 plants for the period studied.[16] The data presented in this study are

[16] *Cost and Margin Trends in the Baking Industry,* Staff Report to the Members of the Committee on Agriculture and Forestry, 85th Congress, 1st Session, Senate Report, May 1, 1957 (Washington, D. C.: U. S. Government Printing Office, 1957).

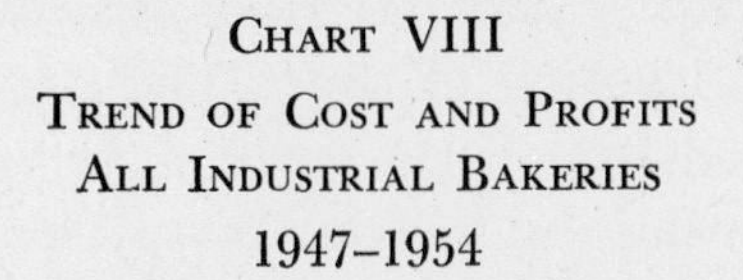

CHART VIII
TREND OF COST AND PROFITS
ALL INDUSTRIAL BAKERIES
1947–1954

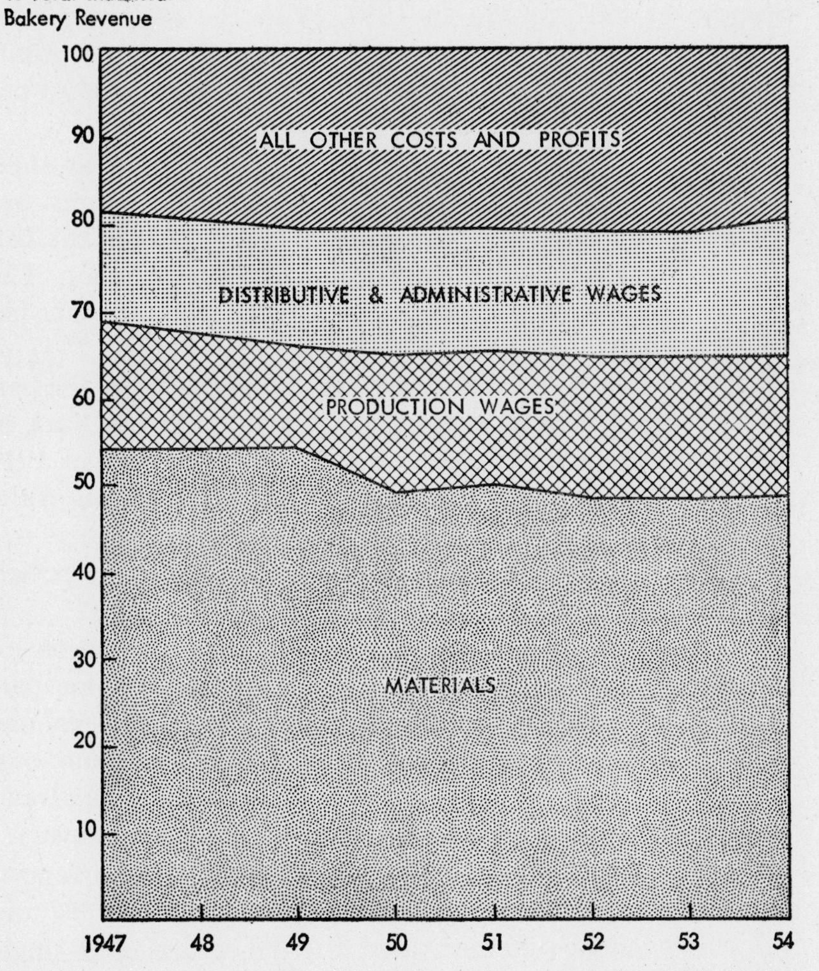

Source: *Census of Manufactures, 1954, Bakery Products,* Bulletin MC-20E, Table 1, *op. cit.*

TABLE 4

18 MULTI-PLANT BAKING COMPANIES: COST OF SPECIFIED ITEMS AND PROFITS AS PERCENTAGE OF SALES 1945 and 1950–55 [a]

Item	*Unit*	*1945*	*1950*	*1951*	*1952*	*1953*	*1954*	*1955*
Number of plants [b]	Number	414	407	405	400	397	411	417
Total Sales	Million $	663.8	986.2	1,094.3	1,149.9	1,205.8	1,273.6	1,348.1
Sales per plant	Thousand $	1,603	2,423	2,702	2,875	3,037	3,099	3,233
Sales	Per cent	100.0	100.0	100.0	100.0	100.0	100.0	100.0
Ingredient cost	" "	37.5	35.6	36.1	34.2	33.8	33.9	32.9
Cost of bakery products bought for resale	" "	.1	.2	.2	.2	.2	.3	.3
Packaging and wrapping material	" "	6.1	6.6	7.4	7.4	7.1	7.1	7.1
Advertising and promotion expense	" "	2.9	2.6	2.5	2.7	2.8	3.0	3.8
Delivery expense, other than wages and salaries	" "	4.6	4.4	4.7	4.9	5.0	4.9	5.0
Wages and salaries of employees	" "	30.7	31.8	31.4	32.2	32.6	32.4	32.7
Fringe benefits to employees	" "	.3	.4	1.0	1.1	1.2	1.3	1.3
Social security taxes	" "	.7	.7	.7	.7	.7	.7	.7
Compensation of officers	" "	.4	.4	.4	.4	.4	.4	.4

Item	Unit	1945	1950	1951	1952	1953	1954	1955
Depreciation allowance	Per cent	1.6	2.2	2.2	2.3	2.2	2.2	2.3
Taxes other than social security, income, and excess profits	" "	.9	.9	.8	.8	.8	.8	.8
Items not specified [c]	" "	5.3	4.9	4.8	4.8	4.8	5.4	5.2
Profits before taxes	" "	8.9	9.3	7.8	8.3	8.4	7.6	7.5
Income and excess profits taxes	" "	5.3	4.2	4.1	4.6	4.4	4.0	3.9
Net profits (after taxes)	" "	3.6	5.1	3.7	3.7	4.0	3.6	3.6

[a] Source: *Cost and Margin Trends in the Baking Industry, op. cit.*

[b] An association of bakeries furnished a combined report for 58 plants of subsidiary companies. This association was counted as 1 company.

[c] Other plant and office expense, including insurance, light and power, fuel, machinery and building repairs, and maintenance, office supplies, and other expense. Computed as a residual (sales less specified costs and profits).

analyzed by Dr. Henry J. Casso, Staff Economist of the Senate Committee on Agriculture and Forestry.

The number of plants remained almost constant, which indicates that there was no marked trend toward consolidation of bakery companies in the period 1945 and 1950–55. However, some companies may have acquired additional plants which they then shut down or liquidated. Also, the companies were not specifically asked to report all plants of companies acquired by mergers so that plants in subsidiary companies may have been omitted. Average sales per plant doubled during the ten year period, from $1.6 million to $3.2 million. Most of this increase represented price rises, so that the actual increase in average volume per plant between 1945 and 1955 was small. (According to the Bureau of Labor Statistics indices, wholesale prices for bakery and cereal products rose about 85 per cent between 1945 and 1955, and prices of bakery products increased relatively more than prices of other cereal products.) "Ingredient costs as a percentage of sales declined from 37.5 per cent in 1945 to 35.6 per cent in 1950 and 32.9 per cent in 1955." [17] The primary reason probably was the relative decline in costs of flour (the principal ingredient used by bakeries) relative to trends in wage rates, cost of packaging materials, and costs of other materials and supplies used by baking companies.

Wages and salaries paid by these baking companies, as a proportion of sales, increased slightly throughout this period —from 30.7 per cent in 1945 to 32.7 per cent in 1955. As a percentage of the gross margin (sales less ingredient costs), however, wages and salaries remained almost constant throughout the period because the gross margin also increased as a percentage of sales. Fringe benefits (pension funds, health and welfare funds, and other nondirect wage payments) reported by these companies increased from 1 per cent of the wage bill in 1945 to 4 per cent in 1955. This is part

---

[17] *Ibid.*

of a general trend in the economy toward increased fringe benefit payments to labor. Social security taxes on wages and salaries were about 2 per cent of the wage bill in each year.

Advertising and promotional expenses tended to increase in recent years at a relatively faster rate than other expenses —increasing from 2.6 per cent of sales in 1950 to 3.8 per cent of sales in 1955.

Other cost items such as packaging and wrapping materials, delivery expense, compensation to officers, depreciation allowances, and taxes made up a relatively stable part of the sales dollar. There was a slight tendency for non-ingredient cost components to increase relative to sales because of the declining proportion represented by ingredient costs.

Total profits of these companies increased over this period but total output apparently did not increase appreciably, leading to the conclusion that profits per unit sold have increased. Profits as a percentage of the sales dollar measure the importance of profits to retail prices or farm-retail price spreads. But rate of profits to sales is not as important a measure of profitability as return on investment. The latter ratio measures the earning power of that part of the total investment in which the stockholder has an interest. Profits and dividends as related to stockholders' equity are discussed later in this report.

Single Plant Companies

> [Table 5] . . . gives a summary of trends in cost and profit items for 18 single-plant companies similar to that given [in Table 4] for multiplant companies. Sales per plant averaged about as high for these companies as for the multiplant companies. The increase in average sales, however, was greater between 1945 and 1955. Cost items as related to sales followed the same general pattern as for the large companies. The only marked exception was in profits, which showed a more or less steady decline in the period 1950–55. Profits as a percentage of sales averaged lower in 1955 than for any other year reported.[18]

[18] *Cost and Margin Trends in the Baking Industry, op. cit.*, pp. 3-6.

TABLE 5

18 WHOLESALE BAKING COMPANIES WITH 1 PLANT EACH: COST OF SPECIFIED ITEMS AND PROFITS AS PERCENTAGE OF SALES, 1945 and 1950–55 [a]

Item	*Unit*	*1945*	*1950*	*1951*	*1952*	*1953*	*1954*	*1955*
Number of plants	Number	18	18	18	18	18	18	18
Total sales	Thousand $	22,187	41,166	46,709	49,909	51,948	55,111	56,157
Sales per plant	"	1,233	2,287	2,595	2,773	2,886	3,062	3,120
Sales	Per cent	100.0	100.0	100.0	100.0	100.0	100.0	100.0
Ingredient cost	" "	42.4	38.2	36.8	36.8	36.1	36.8	36.4
Cost of bakery products bought for resale	" "	1.7	1.8	2.0	2.2	2.4	2.2	2.1
Packaging and wrapping materials	" "	6.3	7.3	7.9	7.7	7.7	7.6	7.7
Advertising and promotion expense	" "	2.0	2.8	2.8	2.9	3.0	3.0	2.9

Item	*Unit*	*1945*	*1950*	*1951*	*1952*	*1953*	*1954*	*1955*
Delivery expense other than wages and salaries	Per cent	5.2	5.4	5.6	5.4	5.5	5.6	6.1
Wages and salaries of employees	" "	24.6	26.3	26.0	27.0	28.0	28.5	28.0
Fringe benefits to employees	" "	.8	.9	.6	.8	.7	.7	.9
Social security taxes	" "	.5	.6	.6	.6	.6	.7	.7
Compensation of officers	" "	2.3	1.8	1.9	1.8	1.8	1.7	1.7
Depreciation allowance	" "	1.7	2.4	2.5	2.6	2.6	2.5	2.6
Taxes other than social security, income, and excess profits	" "	.6	.5	.5	.5	.6	.6	.7
Items not specified [b]	" "	6.9	6.4	8.3	6.9	7.2	6.5	7.2
Profits before taxes	" "	5.0	5.6	4.5	4.8	3.8	3.6	3.0
Income and excess profits taxes	" "	2.1	2.3	2.2	2.6	2.1	1.9	1.6
Net profits, after taxes	" "	2.9	3.3	2.3	2.2	1.7	1.7	1.3

[a] Source: *Cost and Margin Trends in the Baking Industry, op. cit.*

[b] Other plant and office expense, including insurance, light and power, fuel, machinery and building repairs and maintenance, office supplies, and other expense. Computed as a residual (sales less specified costs and profits).

Pursuing the labor cost data presented as part of the total profit and loss analysis above, Chart IX shows the changes in the distribution of the wage dollar for both large multi-plant companies and smaller single plant companies. The wage costs of wholesale baking companies, both multi-plant and single plant, have shifted. Selling and delivery personnel get a larger share of the total wages in 1955 than they did a decade earlier. Moreover, the shift has been more dramatic in the single plant firms; the effect of the trend has been such that the share of the wage bill for production workers has dropped to match the level of multi-plant companies. The average wage cost to land a loaf of bread on the dock is the same ratio of total wage costs for large and for small companies—but sales wages have risen for the single plant firms to well above the ratio of multi-plant companies.

It is important to remember that the absolute wage costs are substantially lower (as a share of the sales dollar) for single plant companies.[19] In 1955 the wage costs (including wages and salaries, fringe benefits and social security taxes) for multi-plant companies were 34.7 per cent of sales, while single plant companies enjoyed a wage cost of only 29.6 per cent of sales.[20] Nonetheless, wage costs as a percentage of the total dollar sales rose more rapidly from 1945 to 1955 for the single plant company: a 3.7 per cent increase for the single plant companies versus a 3 per cent increase for multi-plant companies.

The report shows the trend of ingredient costs over this period for 12 large baking companies (Table 6). Ingredient costs as a percentage of bread sales fell from 42.7 per cent in 1945 to 35.8 per cent in 1955. It is interesting that the trend, though not complete for each year, appears to have been nearly constant. No sharp jumps are indicated for the period

---

19 It should be pointed out that the higher management costs (1.3% of sales greater for single plant companies than for multi-plant companies) cause wages and profits to be smaller items and explain a part of the difference in wage costs and profit levels for the two groups of bakeries.

20 *Ibid.*, p. 6.

CHART IX
WAGES AND SALARIES OF PRODUCTION, DELIVERY AND OTHER EMPLOYEES
1945 and 1950–55

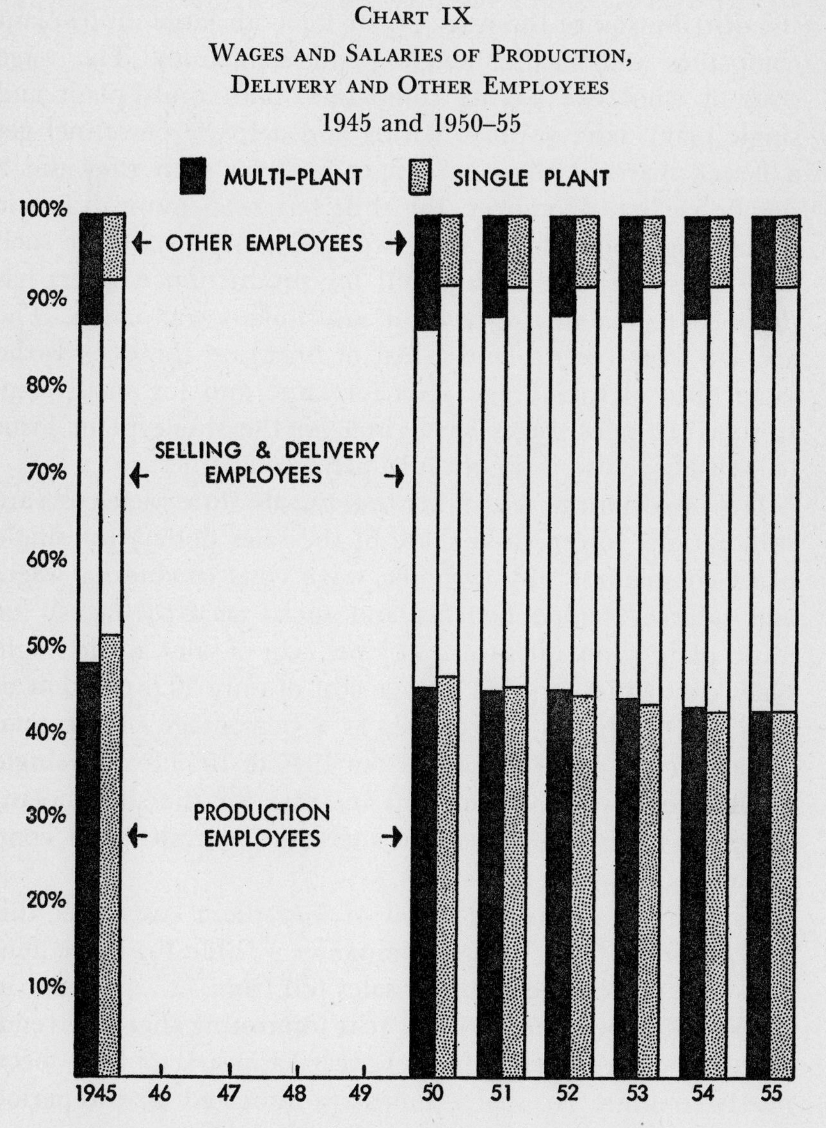

Source: *Cost and Margin Trends in the Baking Industry, op. cit.*

TABLE 6

COST OF FLOUR AND OTHER INGREDIENTS AS A PERCENTAGE OF SALES OF BREAD AND OTHER BAKERY PRODUCTS, 1945 AND 1950–55 *

Year Reported	*1945*	*1950*	*1951*	*1952*	*1953*	*1954*	*1955*
Bread Costs							
12 Large Baking Companies							
Flour	28.2	28.1	27.1	26.2	25.5	26.0	25.3
Other Ingredients	14.5	11.6	12.3	11.6	11.2	11.3	10.5
Total Ingredient Cost as a % of Sales	42.7	39.7	39.4	37.8	36.7	37.3	35.8
14 Single Plant Baking Companies							
Flour	28.2	26.6	25.9	25.3	24.7	25.5	25.3
Other Ingredients	16.2	12.8	13.9	13.9	13.1	13.3	13.1
Total Ingredient Costs as a % of Sale	44.4	39.4	39.8	39.2	37.8	38.8	38.4
Other Bakery Products							
12 Large Companies							
Flour	8.9	8.8	8.8	8.7	8.0	7.8	8.0
Other Ingredients	23.7	21.9	23.4	21.2	22.2	22.3	21.7
Total	32.6	30.7	32.2	29.9	30.2	30.1	29.7
14 Single Plant Companies							
Flour	6.8	8.2	9.1	9.5	9.3	9.1	8.8
Other Ingredients	38.1	33.4	31.5	29.0	29.1	28.5	26.0
Total ingredient costs as a percentage of sales	44.9	41.5	40.6	38.5	38.4	37.6	34.8

* Source: *Cost and Margin Trends in the Baking Industry, op. cit.*, pp. 9-10.

of controlled prices of the Korean War. The sharpest drop has been for ingredients other than flour, i.e., shortening, sugar, milk, etc. Two explanations can be offered: first, the prices of these ingredients have fallen behind the prices of other inputs, particularly labor costs and flour costs, which would tend to drop them as a percentage, and second, bakers have made their products using less of these non-flour ingredients. Against this cost experience of large multi-plant companies, it is interesting to contrast the smaller single plant companies. They have experienced flour cost changes roughly equivalent to large firms as a percentage of sales, but the cost of other ingredients has dropped far less over the same span of time.

The trends for non-bread items are far less dramatic. Flour cost has declined less, from 8.8 per cent down to 8.0 per cent of sales, while other ingredients have also fallen considerably less for non-bread items, from 23.7 per cent to 21.7 per cent among the multi-plant companies. Single plant companies show some slight increase in flour cost as a per cent of sales and a higher average cost of sales other than flour. A similar drop in the cost of non-flour ingredients has been experienced by the smaller firms, from 38.1 per cent of sales to 26 per cent of sales. Product mix differences can well explain most of the variation in cost level between multi-plant and single plant companies, but the sharper falling trend of the single plant companies reveals a shift of product toward that which more closely approximates those offered by multi-plant firms.

The information presented in the first part of this report reveals changes in the environment of the baking industry, that is, cost and demand for bakery products and the distributive channels employed by the industry. Now let us turn to what effects these changes have had on the structure of the industry and its operations.

PART **2**

THE ADAPTING STRUCTURE OF THE BAKING INDUSTRY

THE EXTERNAL PRESSURES described in the previous section have changed the demand for sellers of each type. Some firms, due to forces beyond their immediate control, prosper because of shifts in consumption and shopping habits; others lose volume and face higher costs. Ultimately these changes in cost and output demanded cause changes in the structure of the industry.

Chart X presents a comparison of the number of plants and the dollar value of shipment of bakery products for the years 1947 as opposed to 1954. In the aggregate the number of plants classified as industrial baking plants dropped nearly 700 during the period of eight years. The experience of individual segments is not uniform. The chain store bakeries increased from 90 to 142, a 57 per cent increase in the number of plants, while home service bakeries declined from 624 down to 217 during this same eight year period, a decline of 65 per cent. The change for wholesale bakeries was much less dramatic—an 8 per cent increase or slightly over 400 more wholesale baking plants in 1954 than in 1947. The experience of multi-unit bakery operations is not clearly discernible from the Census data, because the same basis of classification was not employed in the two years studied. The

Chart X

Comparison of Numbers of Plants and Dollar Value of Shipments for Industrial Bakeries

1947–1954

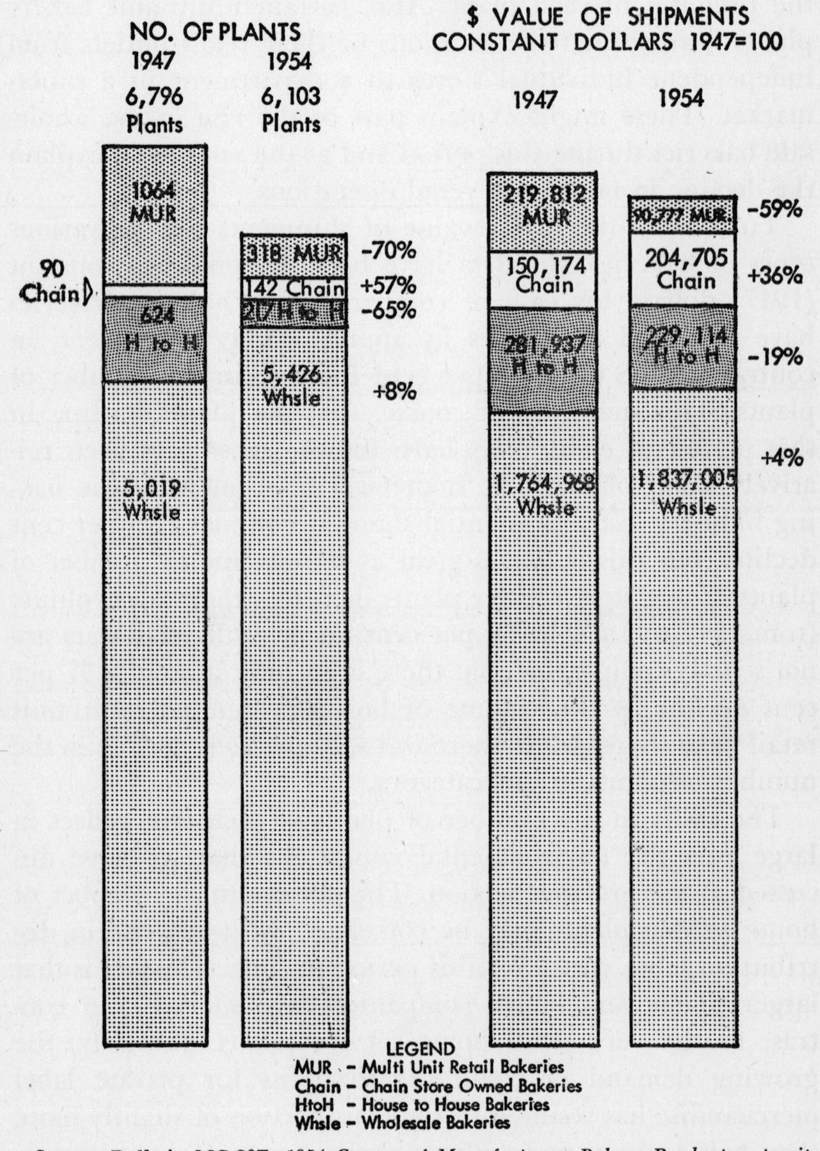

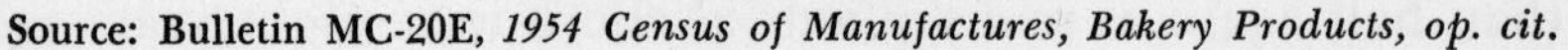

Source: Bulletin MC-20E, *1954 Census of Manufactures, Bakery Products, op. cit.*

drop from over 1,000 multi-unit retail bakeries down to slightly more than 300, or a 70 per cent drop in the number of multi-unit retail bakery plants, reflects in large part a change in classification to exclude bakeries that have some baking on the premises of each plant. Also, certain multi-unit bakery plants have shifted the locations of their retail outlets from independent individual stores to a department in a supermarket. These might explain part of the rise in the wholesale bakeries during this period and at the same time explain the decline in multi-unit retail operations.

Turning to the dollar value of shipments for the various types of bakeries, the data have been presented in constant (1947) dollars for ease of comparision. Wholesale bakeries have increased their sales by approximately 4 per cent, in contrast to the nearly 8 per cent increase in the number of plants. This indicates, of course, that the plants starting in this period of eight years have for the most part been relatively small plants. The home service segment of the baking industry lost a substantial share of volume, a 19 per cent decline, but this is not as great as the decline in number of plants. Chain store captive plants increased their sales volume from 1947 to 1954 by 36 per cent. Multi-unit retail data are not strictly comparable, but there is an indication of a 57 per cent decline in the volume of business done by multi-unit retail bake shops, while there was a 70 per cent decline in the number of plants in this category.

The shifts in the number of plants of each type reflect in large part the environmental conditions that we have discussed in the previous section. The decline in the number of home service plants may be correlated with the rise in distribution labor costs over this period of time. The fact is that larger plants and larger companies have survived, in contrast to the very small home service plants. Similarly, the growing demand of chain organizations for private label merchandise has resulted in the construction of slightly more than half again as many plants as there were eight years ago.

It is interesting that the growth in chain store owned bakery plant sales volume did not match the growth in the number of plants, indicating that the plants constructed in the last eight years have for the most part been small bakery plants.

The shifts in dollar sales volume over the years from 1947 to 1954 give some indication of the structural change, but a more detailed appraisal of these shifts can be gained by study of the per capita sale of specific product classes by each segment. Chart XI shows the per capita output of bakery products for each sales segment for the two years 1947 and 1954.

White bread sales have declined for all segments except food chain plants. In contrast, variety bread output has gone up, on a per capita basis, for all classes of plants except multi-outlet retail and home service. The industry total, however, does not show a net gain for all bread sales; the 2.3 pounds per year per capita gain for variety bread is not sufficient to offset the 5.9 pounds per year per capita decline for white bread.

The sweet goods per capita output has fallen for the industry as a whole and for all segments except chain store captive plants.

The multi-unit-retail bake shops undoubtedly have not suffered the loss indicated in Chart XI, for the change in a classification has upset comparisons. Ignoring this one segment of the industry, comparisons can be drawn about other types of bakeries.

Differences in price levels obscure comparisons made on the basis of sales dollars, but the changes in pounds of output permit meaningful comparisons. The industry per capita poundage output compared here has declined by 6 per cent. But chain captive plants had a per capita increase of 34 per cent; others declined, wholesalers by 4.5 per cent, home service by 23 per cent, multi-unit retail by 48 per cent.

There can be little question that this information demonstrates that baking is an industry with urgent problems,

CHART XI

PER CAPITA OUTPUT OF BAKERY PRODUCTS, 1947 vs. 1954, AMONG VARIOUS SEGMENTS OF THE BAKING INDUSTRY

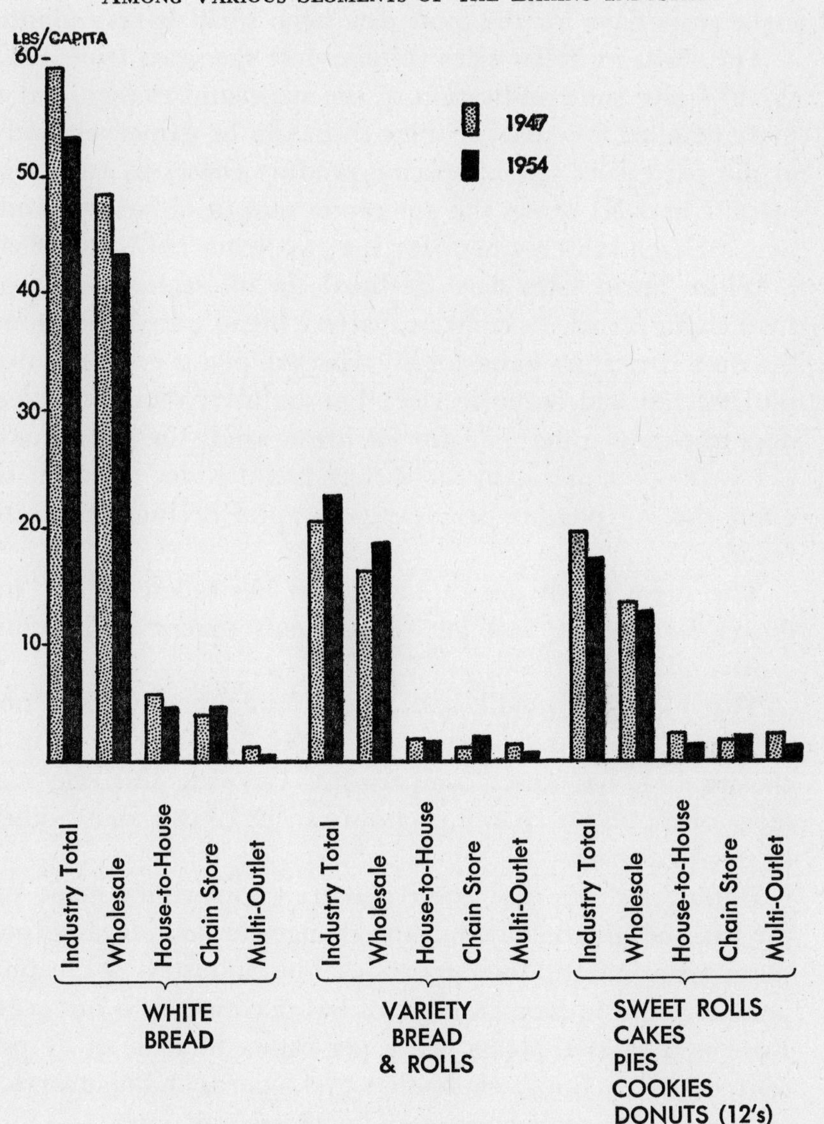

Source: Bulletin MC-20E, *1954 Census of Manufactures, Bakery Products, op. cit.*

made evident by the loss of volume to other food processors at the rate of almost 1 per cent a year.

Shifts in Concentration of Output Among Plants and Firms

The changes among segments of the industry are important in the shifting competitive patterns, but of equal interest are the shifts within each segment—the measures of inter-segment rivalry. Two items of information are available that cast considerable light on these shifts: first, changes in the share of output in plants of various sizes, and second, a special company concentration study done for this study by the Bureau of the Census.

Charts XII, XIII, and XIV show the percentage share of output of three segments of the baking industry done by plants of various sizes (in terms of the number of employees). Chart XII shows that by 1954 a slight concentration had occurred from 1947 in the wholesale bakery segment. In other words, large plants controlled a larger share of total output than they did in 1947. Plants with 425 employees or more controlled 8 per cent more of the output in 1954, plants with 175 employees or more controlled 9 per cent more of output. This shift in concentration is not great when one recalls the technical changes that have emerged and the declining per capita sales of bakery products.

Among the very large home service plants the share of sales volume has risen. Plants with 750 employees or more have gained 10 per cent, from about 33 per cent up to almost 44 per cent of the segment's dollar value added. We know from previously cited data that home service bakeries have lost ground, but this reveals that most of the losses have been among the smaller plants.

Chain store captive bakery plants have experienced just the reverse situation; now large plants control less output than they did in 1947. In 1947 plants with more than 175 employees controlled 83 per cent of the segment's output; in

CHART XII
CONCENTRATION OF OUTPUT
IN WHOLESALE BAKERIES
(1947 compared with 1954)

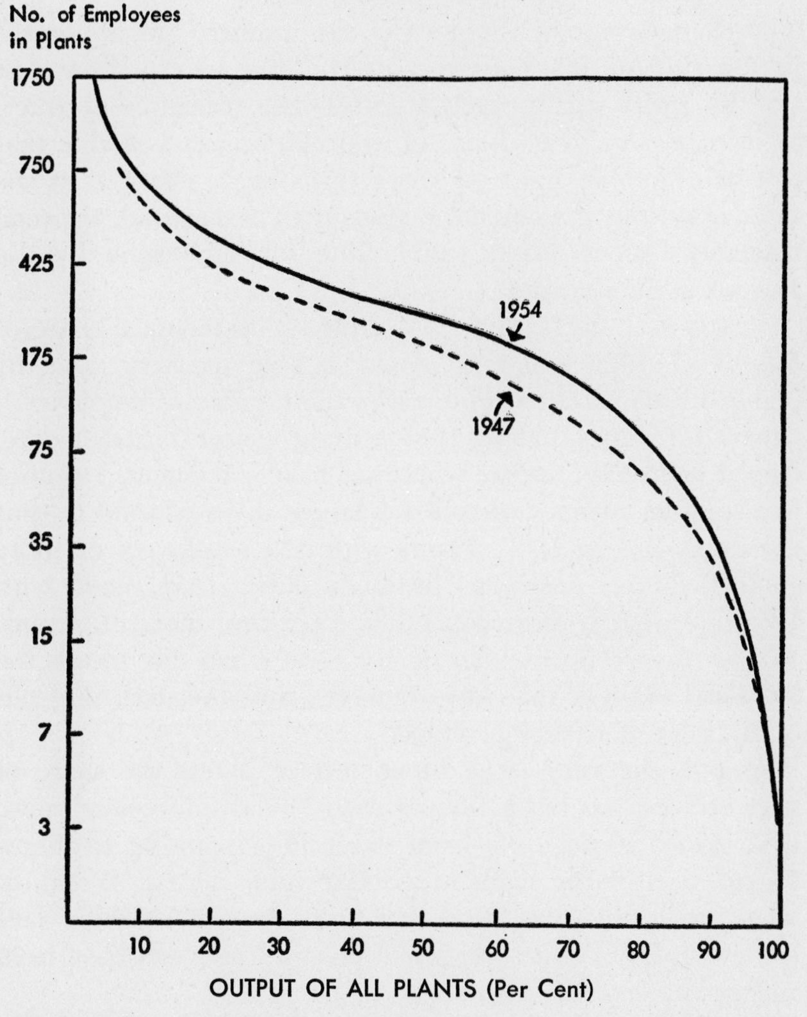

Source: Bulletin MC-20E, *1947* and *1954 Census of Manufactures, Bakery Products,* Table 4, *op. cit.*

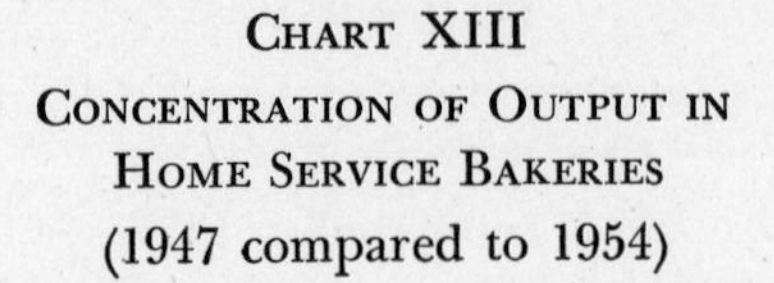

CHART XIII
CONCENTRATION OF OUTPUT IN HOME SERVICE BAKERIES
(1947 compared to 1954)

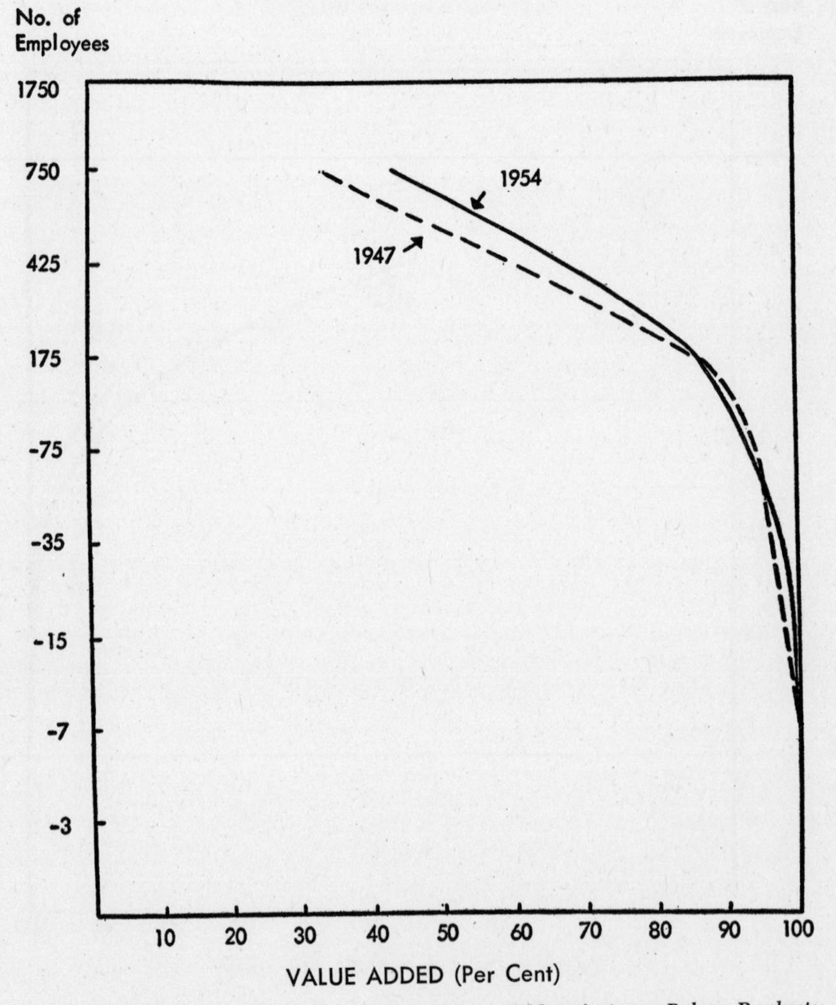

Source: Bulletin MC-20E, *1947* and *1954 Census of Manufactures, Bakery Products,* Table 4, *op. cit.*

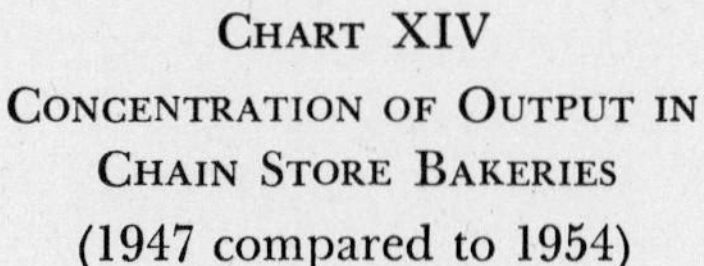

CHART XIV
CONCENTRATION OF OUTPUT IN
CHAIN STORE BAKERIES
(1947 compared to 1954)

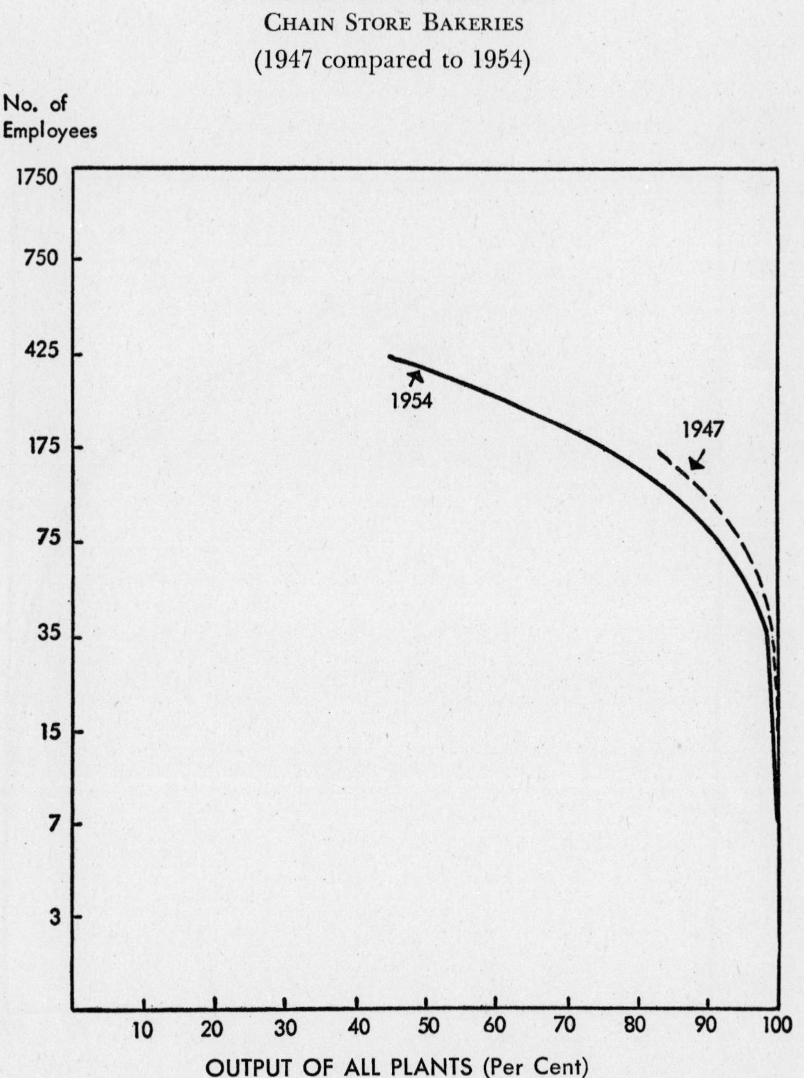

Source: Bulletin MC-20E, *1947* and *1954 Census of Manufactures, Bakery Products,* Table 4, *op. cit.*

1954 these larger plants controlled about 75 per cent of the output.

In brief, the two segments that have lost ground in the share of output have tended toward concentration in larger plants, while chain store captive plants have gained share and new plants seemingly have been smaller than average.

The analysis of structural changes has thus far centered on the distributive segments as a whole and upon the plants within segments. Another facet of the changes is that concerned with company results. Have companies that own many plants fared better than small companies controlling one or a few plants? Which sizes of firms are prospering, large or small?

A special tabulation was made of the *1954 Census of Manufactures* data to permit comparison with a similar analysis from the 1947 census (See Tables 7 and 8).

A comparison of the number of plants owned by firms of different sales volume in 1947 and 1954 is presented below. Looking first at the data on all plants, it can be seen that

TABLE 7

SIZE OF FIRMS RELATED TO PLANTS CONTROLLED
1947 CONTRASTED WITH 1954 *

Company Sales	*Number of Plants*									
	All Plants		*Wholesale*		*Chain*		*H-to-H*		*MU-Ret.*	
	'47	*'54*	*'47*	*'54*	*'47*	*'54*	*'47*	*'54*	*'47*	*'54*
$0-100M	3754	3307	2712	3124	7	15	409	38	626	131
$100M-999M	2401	1768	1817	1482	30	34	150	103	404	155
$1 Mil to 4 Mil	573	395	453	242	46	11	47	39	27	25
Over $4 Mil	69	633	37	492	7	82	18	37	7	7

* Source: Special Tabulations of the 1947 and 1954 *Census of Manufactures.* 1947 tabulations were reported in *Baking in America, op. cit.*

TABLE 8

SIZE DISTRIBUTION OF COMPANIES IN THE PERISHABLE BAKERY PRODUCT INDUSTRY, 1947 AND 1954 *

	Number of Plants											
Number of Plants in Co.	*Number of Companies*		*All Plants*		*Wholesale*		*Chain*		*House-to-House*		*Mutual-Unit Retail*	
	'47	*'54*	*'47*	*'54*	*'47*	*'54*	*'47*	*'54*	*'47*	*'54*	*'47*	*'54*
1	5837	5365	5837	5365	4375	4871	7	52	573	174	882	281
2–7	125	86	363	252	251	123	10	27	25	24	76	28
8–19	14	11	188	134	190	112	38	30	11	19	15	9
20 or more	9	8	409	353	203	260	35	33	15	—	90	—

* Source: Special Tabulations of the 1947 and 1954 *Census of Manufactures*. 1947 tabulations were reported in *Baking in America, op. cit.*

the larger companies (over $4,000,000 in annual sales) have gained substantially in the number of plants controlled, from 69 to 633. In contrast, the other two groups of medium size firms have faced approximately a one-third reduction in the number of plants controlled, while the very small firms (under $2,000 a week in sales) have experienced a one-fifth cut in the number of plants controlled.

The general price level increases have been of the order of 30 per cent from 1947 to 1954, so one would have expected a uniform increase in the number of plants in the successively higher sales volume groupings. This was not so; thus, it becomes apparent that only the very large firms have been able to prosper fully in this seven year period.

Looking across at the data for each segment, it is apparent that plants controlled by larger firms have grown in importance in all segments except multi-unit retail bakeries. The medium-sized firms have lost control of plants, and among wholesale and chain store plants, both the very small firms and large firms have gained control of plants. Small home service firms have experienced a radical fall-off during this time. While a less reliable comparison is shown for multi-unit retail, small firms here have lost ground too.

Before drawing together the implications of these data, there is another set of information based on the same company tabulations, the number of plants in companies owning various numbers of plants (See Table 8). The industry as a whole shows that there has been a small drop in the number of companies owning one or a few plants. Moreover, there has been a slight shrinkage in the number of plants controlled by companies of all sizes, measured by the number of plants owned.

Wholesale bakeries, of course, dominate the industry, and here their experience follows closely the experience of the industry as a whole. In contrast, chain store bakeries have shown an increase in single plant operation, while both home service and multi-outlet bakeries show a substantial drop in the number of small firm plants, and a significant decline in large firm plants.

Another aspect of the same data is revealed in a study of the share of volume controlled by relatively large firms.

Large firms, over $4,000,000 in sales, control over 50 per cent of all sales. Slightly more than half of all sales among wholesale plants are controlled by large companies (51.5 per cent). Yet among grocery chain bakeries, 88 per cent of all sales are controlled by large firms, and nearly 70 per cent of all home service bakery sales are controlled by large firms. Large firms in the multi-outlet retail segment control 40 per cent of sales.

In summary, the big plant and the big company have sustained their position while the small plants and companies have not done as well. The conclusion to be drawn is that the decline in per capita sales has hit hardest at the small plant and firm, particularly home service and multi-unit retail.

Another point of evidence about structural changes is contained in the Senate Report, *Cost and Margin Trends in the Baking Industry.*[1] This is a comparison of sales, investment, profits and dividends for large and small companies. Table 9 presents multi-plant company operations.

This information is described by the report as follows:

> Both sales and investment for the 18 large companies doubled between 1945 and 1955. The ratio of sales to investment has remained rather stable since 1950, ranging between 4.1 and 4.4, compared with 4.7 in 1945. Depreciation allowance in 1955 was almost three times the amount in 1945. Ratio to investment remained relatively stable at 9.1 to 9.7 per cent from 1950 to 1955; depreciation allowance was 7.3 per cent of investment in 1945.
>
> The net profits to sales ratio was the same in 1954 and 1955 as in 1945—3.6 per cent. The largest ratio, 5.1 per cent, was in 1950. This was the last year of five (1946–50) in which profit ratios generally were high compared with periods before and

[1] *Cost and Margin Trends in the Baking Industry, op. cit.*

TABLE 9

BAKING COMPANIES WITH MORE THAN 1 PLANT: SALES, STOCKHOLDERS' EQUITY, INVESTMENT, PROFITS AND DIVIDENDS, 1945 AND 1950–55 [a]

Item	*1945 (414 plants)*	*1950 (407 plants)*	*1951 (405 plants)*	*1952 (400 plants)*	*1953 (397 plants)*	*1954 (411 plants)*	*1955 (417 plants)*
				Million dollars			
Sales	663.8	986.2	1,094.3	1,149.9	1,205.8	1,273.6	1,348.1
Stockholders' Equity	229.0	334.0	343.5	355.0	366.9	386.5	401.9
Investment [b]	140.7	239.7	258.9	269.1	273.7	294.5	310.6
Depreciation Allowance	10.3	21.8	24.3	26.1	26.7	27.8	30.5
Net Profits (After Taxes)	23.7	50.3	40.1	42.3	48.4	45.9	48.4
Dividends	18.5	30.5	30.1	30.5	30.2	30.9	34.1
				Per cent			
Net Profit as Percentage of Sales	3.6	5.1	3.7	3.7	4.0	3.6	3.6
Net Profit as Percentage of Stockholders' Equity	10.3	15.1	11.7	11.9	13.2	11.9	12.0

[a] Source: *Cost and Margin Trends in the Baking Industry, op. cit.*

[b] Total investment in plant and equipment less reserves for depreciation.

since. Net profits after taxes as percentage of stockholders' equity were also higher in 1950 than in other years summarized. With the exception of 1950, there was little change in this ratio. For four of the years the ratio varied only from 11.7 to 12.0 per cent, compared with 10.3 per cent in 1945 and 13.2 per cent in 1953.

Dividends have declined relative to sales—from 3.1 per cent of sales in 1950 to 2.5 per cent in 1955. The proportion of net profits paid out in dividends was 60 per cent in 1950 and 75 per cent in 1951, with later years falling between these percentages. In 1945, dividends were 78 per cent of net profits.[2]

The experience of 18 single plant companies is presented in Table 10. The analytical summary of these data presented in the report was:

> In 1950–55 sales ranged from 318 to 4.7 times the amount of investment in plant and equipment (less reserves for depreciation) for 17 single-plant companies, compared with 6.5 per cent in 1945.
>
> Sales of the single-plant companies increased by about the same percentage as sales of the larger companies between 1950 and 1955, but net profits declined. The ratio of net profits to sales was 1.9 per cent in 1955 compared with 2.4 per cent in 1950. The ratio of net profits to stockholders' equity declined during the same period from 15.7 to 7.9 per cent, compared with 11.2 per cent in 1945. One of the largest of these 17 companies operated 2 plants in 1950–55 and only 1 in 1945.
>
> The proportion of net profits paid out in dividends is much less for the single-plant companies than for the larger companies, ranging from 26 to 29 per cent during 1951–55. The percentages are low, partly because a number of the companies reported no dividends paid.[3]

The high sales to investment ratio of 1945 for both groups of companies reflects the fact that plants had been depreciated during World War II without replacement. By 1950

[2] *Ibid.*, p. 7.
[3] *Ibid.*, pp. 7-8.

TABLE 10

BAKING COMPANIES WITH 1 PLANT EACH: SALES, STOCKHOLDERS' EQUITY, INVESTMENT, PROFITS AND DIVIDENDS, 1945 AND 1950–55 [a]

Item	*1945*	*1950*	*1951*	*1952*	*1953*	*1954*	*1955*
				Thousand dollars			
Sales	26,962	52,187	58,077	61,584	64,306	68,896	71,165
Stockholders' Equity	5,671	11,921	13,034	13,880	15,066	16,257	17,316
Investment [b]	4,176	13,697	14,155	13,037	15,551	15,510	16,099
Depreciation Allowance	465	1,255	1,483	1,574	1,674	1,679	1,748
Net Profits (After Taxes)	636	1,874	1,489	1,460	1,343	1,420	1,363
Dividends	113	307	384	393	386	389	398
				Per cent			
Net Profit as Percentage of Sales	2.4	3.6	2.6	2.4	2.1	2.1	1.9
Net Profit as Percentage of Stockholders' Equity	11.2	15.7	11.4	10.5	8.9	8.7	7.9

[a] 12 wholesale, 1 wholesale and retail, 1 retail, and 3 home-delivery companies. 1 home-delivery company had 2 plants in each year except 1945, as reported in *Cost and Margin Trends in the Baking Industry, op. cit.*

[b] Total investment in plant and equipment less reserves for depreciation.

this had begun to stabilize at a lower ratio, meaning more net investment to produce sales volume in these later years. The larger multi-plant companies never enjoyed as high a ratio during the war, nor have they made as large a relative investment since the war. This corroborates the earlier data that large companies are holding up their market share better than small firms in the period between 1947 and 1954.

If it is assumed that the prices of items of invested capital and bakery product prices moved together over this period and further assumed that these plants are typical in their experience over this period, we can draw further conclusions about the relative successes of large and small firms. The profit on sales of large firms has remained stable, while small firms have lost ground.

In considering the structural changes seen in the evidence presented here, these points should be kept in mind:

1. The cost experience of bakeries has meant a shift in expenditure from ingredients and materials to higher wages for more employees, particularly distribution employees.
2. The chain captive plants have gained in share of sales at a rate that is in sharp contrast to the decline in sales of home service and multi-unit retail bakeries.
3. Large plants have gained share in all segments except chain captive plants.
4. Large companies have gained in share of volume and also gained in relative profitability as small firms have become less profitable.

PART 3

THE EVOLVING COMPETITIVE PATTERNS OF THE INDUSTRY

THE SHIFTS observed in the structure of the industry are the result of competitive activities designed to maximize profit. The struggle for profit and for market position means, in this industry of relatively stable demand, that some firm or segment of the industry loses to balance the others' gains.

Price Changes as Competitive Tools

There have been changes in price and margin structure since 1947. Table 11 presents a comparison of average prices reported in the Census.[1] White pan bread prices rose 40 per cent for wholesale bakers, but only 17 per cent for grocery chain bakeries. Home service bakeries showed the greatest actual price rise, but starting at a higher level the percentage increase was 39 per cent.[2]

The price increase for sweet goods was 42 per cent for wholesale bakeries but an actual decline for grocery chain bakeries of 1 per cent. Home service bakeries increased sweet goods prices by only 21 per cent over this period.

---

1 The Census reports give value of shipments and total pounds for several product classes. Average prices for segments of the industry are computed from these data.

2 Typically, home service bakeries charge the prevailing retail price of wholesale brands. The difference reflects the retail margin for wholesale brands, plus the fact that home service bakeries may not be operating in all markets reported for wholesale bakeries.

TABLE 11

COMPARISON OF PRICE PER POUND OF SELECTED BAKERY PRODUCTS 1947–1954 *

	Industry Total		*Wholesale*		*Grocery Chain*		*House-to-House*		*Multi-Outlet*	
Product	*1947*	*1954*	*1947*	*1954*	*1947*	*1954*	*1947*	*1954*	*1947*	*1954*
White Pan Bread	11.0¢	15.1¢	10.9¢	15.2¢	9.7¢	11.4¢	12.5¢	17.4¢	11.3¢	14.6¢
Sweet Yeast Goods	29.8	37.2	26.2	37.2	29.1	28.9	35.8	43.5	35.8	39.4
Soft Cake	32.1	35.3	30.6	34.4	NA	30.4	38.0	48.0	39.8	43.0
Pies	24.4	25.6	23.0	25.2	NA	26.6	34.2	35.8	30.2	23.6
Donuts (dozens)	25.9	30.2	25.7	30.9	NA	20.5	38.4	43.6	30.1	34.5

* Source: *Census of Manufactures, 1954, Bakery Products,* Bulletin MC-20E, Table 6A, *op. cit.*

Evidently the wholesale bakers have felt both the increasing pressures of costs and of low demand elasticity for their products. In light of the growth of chain store controlled label sweet goods products, it is doubtful that the price spread is likely to continue expanding.

The most important competitive changes involve realignment of distributive systems. Seemingly, these changes stem from the willingness of food retailers to assume more of the distributive functions for bakery products than formerly. There is a growing recognition that food retailers must supply more than just place utility for foods. Distance from the store is not the deciding factor in consumer selection of stores. Overall average cost pricing with promotional leaders offered to attract trade has become very important in food store merchandising.

In order to differentiate their offering and supply one-stop shopping, food store organizations have asked the baking industry for (1) private or controlled label bread and other packaged bakery goods at prices that allow non-integrated stores to meet integrated food chain price competition, and (2) inclusion of service or self-service pastry and hand shop bakery product departments in large stores.

These key demands have emerged during a period of rising labor costs which have increased the problem of maintaining the efficiency of older distributive systems. A further complication has been the existence of potential excess capacity in existing plants. This has created a highly unstable marketing system and produced distributive changes. Here is some of the evidence now available.

First, a number of multi-outlet retail bakeries have shifted their locations from individual stores into space inside supermarkets. This has given them greater traffic at lower overhead.[3] A great many of the multi-outlet bakeries, both in individual stores as well as in supermarkets, have converted

[3] Important examples of this movement are the Awrey Bakeries of Detroit, Van de Kamp of southern California, Ortman's of Omaha, and Burny Brothers of Chicago.

their operations to self-service. This is reported to have cut sales expenses by 10 per cent of the sales price of most items. Many supermarket organizations have established or acquired hand shop bakery facilities to serve their stores. The relatively low capital outlays needed and the absence of serious distribution labor difficulties have facilitated chain store movement into this kind of operation. This type of operation has so far been restricted to the larger stores (over $25,000 retail sales a week). The response of the baking industry has been orderly, and few wasteful costs have been incurred (such as price wars, or intensified promotion directed against competitors' positions rather than against consumer apathy in face of extended product offerings).

The competitive interactions that have resulted from food store demands for lower priced bread (with fewer distributive functions performed by the bakery) have been more complex. For a variety of reasons, bread bakeries have resisted the change in terms of sale and price.

(1) In most markets the Teamsters Union contract for driver salesmen specifies that commissions must be paid on all sales "within the salesman's territory." When food stores request dock delivery, liability for the salesmen's commissions is an open question, a question usually to be decided by arbitration.

(2) The distribution costs incurred to provide route salesmen's service to retail stores is a relatively fixed cost.[4] When the chain of stores is withdrawn from contributing revenue to meet this sales cost, the cost continues.

(3) The wholesale baker who attempts to sell to one chain group of food stores may find other food stores, served by the traditional methods, distressed at the favoritism shown. The baker could suffer some loss of shelf position in the stores not favored by a drop shipment program. Such business risk is not taken lightly when the bakery is limited in the radius from which its customers must come.

[4] Route salesmen's minimum guaranteed wages range up to $100 per week; truck operating costs and supervision remain fixed regardless of sales level.

(4) The present system allows three to ten bakery suppliers to display their goods in each unaffiliated store in the area. The market shares are small, and usually the plants bake fresh products shortly before delivery. As a result the present sales system supports quite a number of plants in each market, some with considerable unused capacity.[5] A shift to drop shipment encourages the food retailer to take most of the display for his own brand.[6] This limits the market outlets for wholesale bakers and threatens the very existence of high cost operators.

These four reasons have had little effect on the intense demands of grocers and their warehouses. Grocers in many markets have continued to try to secure bread on such terms as they can meet the vertically integrated chains.

No clear pattern of competitive response has emerged, but here are some of the actions tried by bakers.

(1) In some markets small plants, operating marginally as traditional wholesale bakers, have been able to operate with the 10 to 12 per cent commission handicap and still provide the retailers with competitively priced bread. Their success hinges on securing larger display areas so that the fixed costs of driver salesmen are spread over a larger quantity of product.[7] Chain stores that do not pay a driver commission still enjoy an advantage, but as long as the distribution costs of the majority of wholesale bakeries are such that the price of advertised brands of bread does not fall, the situation appears to be stable.

(2) Some home service bakeries have established dock sales to

---

[5] In markets where population increases have not kept pace with the national average, and bakeries have improved their production methods to remain competitive, there are plants operating at less than full capacity. Moreover, inexpensively resolved bottlenecks in plants make expanded output possible. Thus, while no nationwide estimate can be developed, many markets seem to have plants with available unused capacity.

[6] Another complicating factor is the extensive sale of yesterday's bakery goods in supermarkets. Overproduction is sold at low prices, creating a secondary market which cuts the average price even below the chain store private label price.

[7] A bakery in Muncie, Indiana, and one in Moline, Illinois, are two successful operations of this type.

food store groups which permit the retail stores to compete effectively with integrated chains. Home service bakeries are in a somewhat better position, for their delivery costs for home service are relatively unaffected as are their relations with other retail food stores (since they would not be likely to have any prior commitment to other food stores). Thus, their only serious problem is to see that the market price for advertised products maintains a level high enough to sustain home service distribution costs. This hinges on abstaining from being indiscriminate in making their program available to all small food organizations. If the program of dock sale was universally available, the market price would likely be affected.

(3) Some tentative steps in the direction of joint action by the bread bakers in particular markets have emerged. If the majority of suppliers is engaged in this program, none will be "blackballed" for failing to offer this service to retailers not able to qualify. Also, the labor situation is more likely to be dealt with effectively in joint action. In contrast, when one supplier asks the union for a contract for hourly rated drivers for drop shipment sales, it embarrasses the union because this may not be granted to all operators (or wanted by all) at the same time. The primary advantage to the joint operation system is that it permits stable market share structure to continue, for each bakery can have a share of sales, just as in the past. High distribution costs remain in the older route selling systems, but there is little that can be done to prevent this cost from rising on a unit basis when volume is diverted from it.

The potentially available capacity in many markets poses a real threat to continued stability.[8] Prime costs (or marginal

[8] Few bread plants are run round the clock, six days a week. Thus, up to the limit of filling up a shift or adding one or two shifts, the increment in cost is slight over the raw materials, supplies and direct labor. Increased investment in plants over the past few years, cited earlier, as well as stable demand have combined to create the potential of excess capacity.

costs) are slightly more than half of the long run average cost for bread products, and the temptation to offer products at less than full cost is growing among marginal producers threatened with extinction.[9]

The problem has been further complicated by the fact that improved roads bring the housewife to the larger, more distant stores and also bring large bread trucks from other nearby cities, formerly in isolated bakery markets.

The conclusions about major competitive changes are:

(1) The inroads of pastry departments in stores are likely to affect the structure of multi-outlet retailers, forcing many to move their retail outlets into large food stores.

(2) The growing demands of food retail and wholesale organizations for dock delivery at lower prices pose a threat to the traditional distributive system of wholesale bakers. The gains in economies of distribution via dock selling will have corollary changes in production centers for bread. Fewer plants, with low production costs, will be maintained under the emerging system. Since few small bread plants enjoy alternative uses of a profitable sort, the struggle to adapt to the new system is likely to produce price wars. The transition can be aided by joint sales programs, provided all suppliers are given the opportunity to participate and the quantity discounts reflect cost differences. In this way transition may be eased, but in the final analysis a fixed market demand and shrinking display opportunity for marginal sellers are an economic game of musical chairs. When capacity utilization again matches market demand and market quality needs, full cost pricing will again be stabilized.[10]

The margin taken by retail food stores selling wholesaler brands of bread has not changed much over the past four years. A grouping of data from 105 markets into the nine

[9] Senate Report, *Cost and Margin Trends in the Baking Industry, op. cit.*

[10] The author would like to stress again at this point that these are his own speculations about the future and his own conclusions, and that these ideas are not to be construed as representing the views of the American Bakers Association.

Census regions shows little change in margin. Only two regions show a change of more than 1 per cent in margin over the period July 1955 to May 1957—New England and the West North Central.

TABLE 12

THE RETAILER MARGIN ON WHOLESALE BRANDS OF WHITE BREAD

Region	*July '55*	*May '56*	*May '57*
East South Central	14.4%	14.2%	14.6%
West South Central	13.6	13.5	13.8
Mountain	16.6	16.5	17.2
Pacific	19.1	19.4	19.5
New England	15.0	15.0	17.1
Middle Atlantic	15.7	15.4	15.8
South Atlantic	14.3	13.8	13.7
East North Central	14.8	14.9	15.5
West North Central	14.8	14.7	15.9

Source: *National Bread Price Surveys,* Anheuser-Busch, St. Louis, Missouri. Reports dated July 1955, May 1956, and May 1957.

There are wide differences among areas of the country, with the Pacific Coast having the highest margins and New England a close second. The South offers retailers the lowest margins.

There appears to be no overall tendency for margins to be related to the spread in price between chain store brands and wholesale brands.[11] It is interesting, however, that price spread gained in New England and the West North Central region parallels the gains in retailer margins. Table 13 presents price spreads in a summary of 95 markets grouped by the Census regions. There has been decline in the average spread between chain brand price and wholesaler brand retail price for white bread in five of the areas. The Pacific and Mountain state markets show the greatest drop.

[11] The correlation between price spread of chain brands and retail margin was r = .09. Based on analysis of 74 markets reported in the May, 1957 Anheuser-Busch *National Bread Price Survey.*

TABLE 13

PER CENT BREAD PRICE SPREAD: WHOLESALE BAKERS' RETAIL PRICES OVER CHAIN RETAIL PRICES *

	July '55	*May '56*	*May '57*	
East South Central	22.7	25.6	19.5	–
West South Central	20.0	24.5	20.8	0
Mountain	22.6	22.6	12.8	–
Pacific	14.0	8.9	8.8	–
New England	33.3	33.3	35.7	+
Middle Atlantic	26.8	37.1	23.4	–
South Atlantic	25.4	28.3	26.7	0
East North Central	26.2	29.8	24.4	–
West North Central	25.2	27.7	28.1	+

* Based on analysis of *National Bread Price Surveys* of Anheuser-Busch, Inc., St. Louis, Missouri.

The absolute level of difference in price is not uniform, and for larger loaf sizes, twenty ounce and one and one-half pound sizes, there is little systematic relationship between price level and the spread between chain store brands and wholesaler brands. In the case of one pound loaf size, 42 markets were analyzed and the results are interesting. There is quite a strong relationship, i.e., the higher the level of wholesaler's price, the greater the spread between chain brands and wholesalers' brands.[12]

[12] The correlation between price spread and price level for one pound white bread was $r = .64$, indicating that the higher the price level of bread for wholesalers, the greater the likelihood that chains would enjoy a wide price spread. The differences in cost structure go a long way to explain this. The production costs are likely to be similar for chains or wholesalers, but distribution costs are different. Analysis based on Anheuser-Busch, *National Bread Price Surveys* of May 1957 and September 1957.

PART | 4

THE CHANGING ECONOMIC RESULTS

ECONOMICS AND MARKET ANALYSIS are not precise tools for observation, and, equally important, they are not precise tools for analysis and judgments of performance. The economic results or performance of an industry must be measured against the whole of society, asking three basic questions:

1.) *Does baking provide the products most wanted in sufficient quantity?* Traditional producing centers seem not to be offering products that will attract higher income families to spend at a rate much higher than low income families. Yet, the number of new products being developed by new entrants from the frozen food fields are capturing a growing share of food dollars. The supply is, then, adequate and with the entry of new forms of product the variety seems to be adapting to new wants.

2.) *Is the baking industry prepared to offer too much product and devoting, therefore, too many resources to supply the need?* a.) The answer seems to be yes. Some of the large bread baking plants seem to be in a position of having capacity that is not fully utilized. b.) Moreover, smaller plants may be in a worse position with respect to unused capacity. Home service bakeries particularly seem to be in this position, even with the sharp decline in the number of operators. c.) It is evident that many plants have experienced idle time before closing their doors. d.) Another factor is the continued substantial investment in plant facilities even though total unit sales have risen only slightly over the decade where investment records are reported.[1]

3.) *Is the cost to consumers "fair"?* a.) The cost of bakery products is excessive if monopoly profits are exacted by manufacturers controlling supply. Our guide must be to evaluate how effective competition operates to restrict monopoly practices. The high degree of market overlap, the intense intersegment rivalry, and the limiting factors of food store owned bakery operations seem to thwart any systematic profiteering. In brief, supply cannot be controlled; thus, effective monopoly action seems to be prevented. b.) The industry is not offering just one product at one set of terms and at one price. c.) The differing distributive services seem today to be important factors of cost that produce differences in price. d.) The industry in many markets is in a transition toward lower distribution costs and fuller plant utilization. This is because the pressures of large food outlets and large food warehouses are for fewer brand offerings and lower distribution costs for all food, bakery goods included. A necessary result is fuller use of fewer plants. e.) As a few plants are squeezed out of operation in various markets, less than average cost pricing is likely to ensue. Eventually bakery product prices may actually fall below the full costs of production and distribution. As marginal plants close, pricing may well then return to full cost.

These specific answers to questions of economic criteria are concise, perhaps to the point of abruptness. A more general statement regarding the changing economic results is appropriate in conclusion. The baking industry, along with several other major food processing industries, faces changes that are induced by the profound revolution in food wholesaling and retailing of the last decade. New methods of distribution are

[1] *Cost and Margin Trends in the Baking Industry, op. cit.,* pp. 6 and 7.

emerging that better satisfy the pressures brought by integrated food warehouses and retail stores. The challenge to the food industry today lies in answering the changed and still changing wants of highly mobile and critical consumers. Baking as an industry offers a wide line at a wide range of prices reflecting differences in service and quality. The industry is responding to these demands to change under the leadership of executives acutely aware of the problems and alert to alternatives. The pressures of price competition come primarily from food retailers who are themselves embattled over the whole range of food and non-food items in a struggle for the consumers' patronage. The transition to lower distribution costs will no doubt be passed through as the business of grocery retailing stabilizes as the number of supermarkets reaches its peak and levels off. In turn, growth opportunities exist as new products and nearly forgotten fine old pastries grow to significant proportions.